# THE CANER'S HANDBOOK

## A Practical Guide to Restoring Cane, Rush and Wicker Furniture

Bruce W. Miller and Jim Widess

COLLINS

Published in 1984
by William Collins Sons & Co., Ltd
London, Glasgow, Sydney,
Auckland, Johannesburg

First published in the USA in 1983 by Van Nostrand
Reinhold Co., Inc.

Copyright © 1983 Van Nostrand Reinhold
Co., Inc.

Designed by Karolina Harris
Photographs by Jim Widess
Line drawings by Bruce Miller

ISBN 0 00 411772 7

Printed and bound in Great Britain by William
Collins Sons & Co., Ltd

# CONTENTS

# ACKNOWLEDGMENTS

I thank Stephanie Greene, who suggested the idea of this book, and my wife Mary Donnelly for her invaluable aid and comfort.

Bruce Miller

We could never have published any of the information in this book if Elaine and David Myers had not asked me to baby-sit for their chair for two years. Lynn Kessner first suggested I change professions, Millie Karlin undertook the venture with me, and Ellen Widess gave me lots of early encouragement. Thank you Sharon Moreland, Kathleen Wilson, Jean Stallcup, Lee Stallcup, Shandra Hoagland, Don Harris, Bill Halprin, Roger Whipple, Bill Fimpler, and Oscar and Emma Hensley for all your patience, energy, lessons, and inspiration.

Thank you Sher for everything. Your love and support through this manuscript was beautiful.

Jim Widess

For assistance in gathering photographs we would like to thank V.S. Agarwal, of the Botanical Survey of India; Bill Fimpler, of Cane and Basket Supply in Los Angeles; and the many clients who unwittingly allowed their chairs to be photographed. The Farm Security Administration photographs are from the Library of Congress collection. The still-life photograph of tools and materials was designed by Sher Lynn Elliott.

We are much indebted to L.H. Burkill, Richard Saunders, Ruth Comstock, and Patricia Corbin for their excellent previous work in this field.

## TECHNICAL NOTE

Some of the items referred to in this book may not be readily available. In these cases, the following alternatives are suggested:

| | |
|---|---|
| Shaker tape | *stout carpet binding tape* |
| Hickory splints | *home-made splints are adequate, or ask your local timber merchant to cut splints to size* |
| Hand clamps | *large mole wrench, or small clamps* |

In addition, the reader may not be familiar with certain terms used by the American authors in this book. The following list should prove helpful:

| | |
|---|---|
| Cattails | *cat's-tail or reed mace* |
| Clippers | *side-cutting pliers* |
| Clothespins | *clothes pegs* |
| Danish cord | *Polycord, cotton cord* |
| Fiber rush | *Polycord, natural rush, seagrass* |
| Ice pick | *bodkin or awl* |
| Mat knife | *lino or Stanley knife* |

| | |
|---|---|
| Needle-nose pliers | *long-nose pliers* |
| Pruning clippers | *secateurs* |
| Pump sprayer | *indoor plant spray* |
| Rawhide | *untanned hide* |
| Tack puller | *tack lifter* |

## MEASUREMENT EQUIVALENTS

1 inch = 25.4 mm
1 mm = 0.039 inch

1 foot = 30.5 cm
1 cm = 0.39 inch

1 yard = 0.914 metre
1 metre = 39.37 inches

1 pound = 0.45 kg
1 kg = 2.2 pounds

The authors have used both metric and imperial measures in the book. The following is a table of approximate equivalents used by the authors as a 'ready reckoner':

| Inches | Millimetres | | Inches | Centimetres | | Feet | Metres |
|---|---|---|---|---|---|---|---|
| 3/64 | 1 1/4 | | 1 | 2.5 | | 1 | 0.3 |
| 1/16 | 1 1/2 | | 2 | 5 | | 5 | 1.5 |
| | 1 3/4 | | 3 | 7.5 | | 10 | 3 |
| 5/64 | 2 | | 4 | 10 | | 15 | 4.5 |
| 3/32 | 2 1/4 | | 5 | 12.5 | | 20 | 6 |
| | 2 1/2 | | 6 | 15 | | 25 | 7.5 |
| 7/64 | 2 3/4 | | 7 | 17.5 | | 30 | 9 |
| 1/8 | 3 | | 8 | 20 | | 40 | 12 |
| 9/64 | 3 1/4 | | 9 | 22.5 | | 50 | 15 |
| 5/32 | 3 1/2 | | 10 | 25 | | 75 | 22.5 |
| 11/64 | 4 | | 12 | 30 | | 100 | 30.5 |
| 3/16 | 4 1/2 | | 15 | 37.5 | | 250 | 75 |
| 13/64 | 5 | | 18 | 45 | | 500 | 150 |
| 7/32 | 5 1/2 | | 20 | 50 | | 1000 | 305 |
| | 5 3/4 | | 24 | 60 | | | |
| 15/64 | 6 | | 36 | 90 | | | |
| 1/4 | 6 1/2 | | 39 | 100 | | | |
| 9/32 | 7 | | | | | | |
| 19/64 | 7 1/2 | | | | | | |
| 11/32 | 8 1/2 | | | | | | |
| 3/8 | 9 1/2 | | | | | | |
| 13/32 | 10 | | | | | | |
| 7/16 | 11 | | | | | | |
| 1/2 | 12 1/2 | | | | | | |
| 9/16 | 14 | | | | | | |
| 5/8 | 15 3/4 | | | | | | |
| 3/4 | 19 | | | | | | |
| 7/8 | 22 | | | | | | |
| 1 | 25 | | | | | | |

# INTRODUCTION

This book is a descriptive guide to the restoration of cane and wicker furniture. Knowing the techniques herein will benefit the experienced craftsman as well as the novice. We try to answer the basic problems encountered in restoring handwoven furniture and to provide clear and simple yet instructive direction for some of the more complex techniques.

*The Caner's Handbook* is a new approach to the traditional art of restoring handwoven chair seats. There are detailed photographs and line drawings side by side with the text. Both the visual and the printed texts move in a descriptive step-by-step motion, outlining the process needed to restore your chair. We thought this method was the most useful way to explain the various styles of hand-weaving described here. The illustrations, then, are not merely supplemental but form an integrated part of the instruction. In fact in many cases the illustrations alone are thorough enough to give even the novice a reasonable grasp of the task at hand. Where necessary, the text and illustrations also show hand and body positions that might otherwise be confusing.

Whether your chair needs cane, wicker, rush, or other restoration, this book places valuable specific information in your hands. The chairs used as examples were chosen to illustrate as wide a range as possible, given the problems encountered in seat weaving.

Although all the examples in this book are chairs, the processes and weaving styles described can be applied to many other types of furniture from—and including—large wicker sofas, rattan chests, and baskets to decorative caned screens.

A special feature of this book, in addition to the usual information available on cane, rush, and splint, is a section with instruction and illustrations on some of the rare cane weaves. Up until now, information on many of these fancy weaves (such as Spider Weave, Snowflake, and Sun Ray) has been difficult to find. Even our search uncovered only one document with explicit instruction on the sunray pattern.

*The Caner's Handbook* also contains extensive chapters on wicker and Danish cord as well as rarely encountered information on binder cane, Shaker tapes, and rawhide weaving. To our knowledge this is the first book to give detailed instruction on both rawhide and Shaker tapes. Our work may be the first treatment of this material in a considerable number of years, or perhaps ever.

We hope that the fresh presentation of this material—which has long been passed on verbally and in the doing of it—has now been preserved in print for those people who don't have access to a master caner. This is not to say that one need be a master craftsman to make use of this book but rather that much of the information presented here was previously unavailable to the public. One should, however, have a certain proclivity toward work and at least a moderate capacity for attention to detail. It has also been suggested that both patience and foresight are key ingredients to successful handweaving.

The book itself is set up in eight chapters, with each detailing a different type of seat weaving. The first chapter is an historical and general introduction to materials, tools, and techniques. Later chapters each begin with a brief introduction to the specific tools and materials needed to complete the work at hand. Questions of alternative styles and processes are also discussed at this point. For example if your chair needs work you will be able to tell if hand caning or machine caning is required. And further, how much work is needed, how much materials cost, whether they are easily obtainable and where they can be purchased. All of these questions are taken up before the instruction begins. Each chapter then goes on to detail a variety of specific techniques relating to the type of chair involved.

*The Caner's Handbook* contains a wealth of traditional craft techniques that will appeal to both amateur and professional craftsmen. The book is especially for people interested in saving money by doing the work themselves. There is great satisfaction to be taken in the successful completion of a project with one's own hands. With *The Caner's Handbook,* anyone can make a chair seat "as good as new."

# Handwoven Furniture

## A BRIEF HISTORY

Man has used wicker objects for millennia. Even today, a number of early specimens survive from the tombs of Egypt, for the dry, static atmosphere of the burial crypts was an excellent preservative. The Egyptian Museum, in Cairo, has several boxes and a chest made from reed, papyrus, and rush. Both Chinese and Sumerian civilizations also record the use of wicker in statuary and early written histories.

Natural-rush seating dates in Egypt from 4000 B.C. It was made, as it is today, from bulrush, marsh flag, or cattail. It was harvested in the late summer or early fall, when the leaves were the longest and before the autumn rains. Leaves were then separated, and dried for several weeks before they were used.

China is thought to be the originator of the caned chair. These chairs were commonly available in the East for many centuries before they were brought westward by the opening of the China Trade.

Cane is the hard outer bark of the rattan palm, the whole stem of which is called rattan. Reed is made from the soft inner core. Wicker is a generic term that covers rattan, willow, and other natural products.

It is difficult to determine which country in Europe first made widespread use of wicker furniture. We do know that both wicker and rush were used in furniture mak-

ing during the Middle Ages. The wicker furniture was usually made from willow or other local woods rather than from rattan.

In the East, products from the rattan palm numbered in the thousands and were used for anything from fish traps to suspension bridges. The word rattan is from the Malay word *rotan*, which means "to pare." Its origin is presumably manifested in the paring or stripping action the rattan undergoes during collection and preparation for market.

In the West, rattan first appeared in Portugal, France, and Britain in the eighteenth century, in the form of crudely caned chairs. The crude, uneven caning on these chairs soon disappeared as Western craftsmen mastered the caning art, and within a hundred years their quality was much improved. The Industrial Revolution brought even more improvements and variety, due largely to a number of specific furniture makers and their inventions.

The first was Cyrus Wakefield, who, during the 1850s, established a factory in Massachusetts for the exclusive purpose of making rattan furniture. South Reading, Massachusetts, later called Wakefield, quickly became one of the major centers of rattan-furniture making in the United States.

At that time the primary material for the construction of rattan furniture was the peel or exterior of the rattan palm, called cane.

The inner reed core was usually thrown out as waste, but Wakefield was the first to make wide use of it. Unlike cane, which could only be polished and lacquered because of its silica surface, the reed core could be both painted and stained. Wakefield used the reed for a number of products including the light hoop frames worn under petticoats and skirts that were fashionable around the time of the Civil War. William Houston, who was employed by Wakefield, invented a manual loom to weave cane webbing. Later, 2 men, Levi Heywood and Gardiner A. Watkins, devised a power loom to weave sheet cane, or close-woven machine cane as it is presently called. Later, Heywood and Cyrus Wakefield formed the Heywood-Wakefield Company, the most important furniture-manufacturing company of this period.

Wicker furniture, aided and improved by 3 inventive men, became enormously popular from the 1860s onward. The versatile rattan lent itself to the ornate Victorian style, a style that culled and borrowed from the past Gothic, Chinese, Rococo, Moorish, Classical, and even Renaissance styles. With this panoply of design to draw upon, wicker designs flourished. One could find a rocker in any style: with a Gothic square, more angular back, and controlled curves or with Rococo flourishes; with bulbous Moorish sides or even with Viennese bentwood or elaborate American rocker styles. Several Heywood-Wakefield catalogs listed over 70 separate rocker designs.

Some Victorian parlor and porch-furniture pieces were literally tortured with arabesques and concentric curves, an indulgence that today seems flamboyant yet fascinating. Rattan was extreme, exotic, and a craze. Victorian wicker porch furniture appeared everywhere. Elaborate fanback or peacock chairs graced the verandas and sun rooms in Britain and America. Reed baby carriages, lamp shades, cribs, rockers, love seats, book cases: all were in use. Complete matching sets (usually including 4 or 5 chairs, a rocker, and a settee) were used to furnish entire rooms. During the 1890s, what were known as Turkish corners were the rage. These normally included a rattan table, a settee, or several chairs. The potted palm *de rigueur!*

Rattan in its natural state did not go unnoticed either. In the February 6, 1897, issue of the *Gardiner's Chronicle*, *Calamus ciliaris* was described as "the most beautiful and useful [species] from a decorative view. . . . It would make an excellent plant for the dinner table, or for an exhibition. . . . When it is about 18 inches in height, it throws out from near the top of the sheath a very slender growth which is covered with numerous small hooked spines to aid the plant in climbing. . . . When used for dinner table decoration, the climbing tails had better be cut off, as they are liable to hang on to anything with which they come into contact."

Another facet of the Victorian style was its fullness. Lounge chairs or settees often featured large cushions surrounded by rolled arms, serpentine in shape. These deep-rolled arms gave way to scrollwork and curlicues, which added to their expansive appearance.

In general, Victorian furniture had beneath its multiple curves and filigree a consummate elegance and integrity. Above all, it had strength and durability, and conveyed a feeling of ease. It reflected not only the excesses of its time but also the burgeoning spirit of the Victorian Age.

Another type of seating dating from the Victorian Era was being made in the Shaker communities. Dating from the 1830s, these Shaker tapes were woven from cotton on a handloom, dyed, and then woven over a cushion or cotton batting to make a durable chair seat.

After the turn of the century, wicker design became more subdued and straightforward. The ornate Victorian aesthetic with its Art Nouveau curves was supplanted by the more angular and vertical Mission style. Unfortunately, a great many of the now out-of-fashion Victorian pieces were simply dismissed to the junk heap and left to perish.

Mission furniture, sometimes called Craftsman after Gustav Stickley, was a quiet revolution in design compared to the exotic abandon of the Victorian Era, for it was based on structural principles rather than decorative styles. The Craftsman period began around 1890 in upstate New York and extended across the United States through the *Craftsman* Magazine (1902 through 1916), written and published by Gustav Stickley. Craftsman furniture tended toward sedate functional pieces. Gone were the high gloss and complexity of earlier days, giving way to a mat finish and strong, relatively pure lines.

The Dryad Works, in England, produced an entire line of gracefully curved yet simple wicker designs. Dryad wicker was inspired by the same functional spirit embodied in Craftsman furniture. It was almost as though the Victorian rage had so muddied the waters with its multifarious use of historical design influences that furniture makers began seeking clarity and simplicity, or what Gustav Stickley called the ''essential bones'' in their designs.

After World War I, fiber rush, a newly invented product, was utilized by the wicker industry. Fiber rush is tough-grade paper fiber twisted into a filament to resemble natural rush. This strand is then woven like natural rush on seat bottoms or strung between rattan posts on chair backs. Sometimes furniture manufacturers went so far as to weave the entire chair, excluding the structural posts, from fiber rush. This made wicker furniture much cheaper (and therefore more affordable to the common man), but unfortunately the quality also suffered.

Designs were curbed to conform to the machines' abilities, and the individuality of the pieces became lost. This widespread use of machine-made products and the introduction of tubular aluminum frames made genuine wicker furniture less profitable and also outmoded. This led to the public's disaffection with the wicker style during the middle 1900s; it has only been in the last 20 years that a great resurgence of interest in natural materials has led to the current mass appeal of wicker and cane.

One could find any number of reasons for this resurrection of interest in handwoven furniture. Oak and wicker furniture have come of age because of their genuine antique value, with many of the pieces over a hundred years old. Another explanation is the high quality of workmanship and materials making restoration preferable to buying new.

Handwoven furniture also represents a link with an older era—a link with our grandparents and great grandparents—and as a natural thing it brings us closer to our roots.

It is also true that Western furniture tastes have influenced Oriental manufacturers so that pieces are now being designed especially for the modern market. Both durability and comfort have been improved with the advent of stronger quality controls. A better product coupled with a low price has created an expanding market.

## CARE OF WOVEN FURNITURE

After you invest much time in your newly acquired skill and bring new life to your woven furniture, you will want it to last as long as possible. Proper care and placement is the key.

Avoid putting cane or wicker in hot, dry, sunny rooms or next to heater outlets. Low-humidity heat will dry out cane and reed and make them brittle. Wicker should be

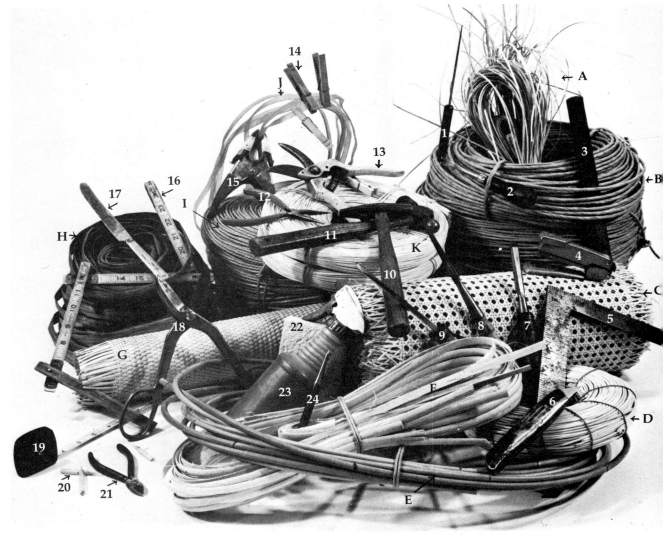

*1-1.* An array of tools and materials: (1) ice pick (2) tack puller (3) rasp (4) stapler (5) square (6) mat knife (7) ¾-inch chisel (8) ⅛-inch chisel (9) screwdriver (10) tack hammer (11) hammer (12) needle-nose pliers (13) pruning clippers (14) clothespins (15) hand clamp (16) carpenter's rule (17) flat kitchen knife (18) tin snips (19) tape measure (20) pegs (21) clippers (22) sponge (23) pump sprayer (24) center punch (A) hank of chair cane (B) coil of fiber rush (C) prewoven cane, open weave (D) coil of round reed (E) coil of rattan (F) ⅜-inch flat oval reed (G) prewoven cane, close woven (H) hickory splint (I) coil of Danish cord (J) half pound of rawhide (K) coils of round reed.

oiled once a year with a mixture of 1 part boiled linseed oil to 1 to 2 parts paint thinner or turpentine. Brush off any dirt with a vegetable brush, and then apply a thin coat of the oil mixture. Varnishing or lacquering wicker is not recommended because it seals the reed and does not allow it to breathe or absorb moisture from the air. Painting, although fashionable, also seals the reed. If you wish to color the reed, an oil stain is the best method to use.

To restore moisture to rattan furniture, you can safely hose it down. But only mist reed-woven wicker, as soaking will raise lots of hairs that will then need to be trimmed

or torched off. Avoid hosing wooden parts at all costs, as wood will swell, possibly split, and warp.

To prolong the life of a caned seat, tighten the cane periodically. Cane has a certain amount of stretch or sag, which allows for the additional stress of someone sitting. After some months of use, cane will begin to lose its "memory" and the sag will remain. When the cane can stretch no more, it will begin to wear against the edge of the chair or strands will break in the center. By rewetting the cane with warm water and a sponge (preferably on the underside, which is not protected by the glossy ba_

*1-2. From left to right: Manau rattan with peel, Manau rattan without peel, Tohiti rattan.*

ting the cane dry slowly overnight, you can restore its original tightness.

Reseal rush every year or so with a thin coat of shellac. Never try to wash a fiber-rush or Danish cord seat: these materials are made from paper, and washing, even with soap suds, will only weaken and fray the fibers. You are much better off sealing the seats first to protect them from spills and dirt and to ensure that a simple brushing or wiping will remove the offending splatter.

Shaker tapes can be washed with soap and water. The whole foam cushion and tapes can be scrubbed and then set out to dry. If your Shaker chair seat is stuffed with the traditional cotton batting, use a minimum of soap and water. Old or antique tapes will not have colorfast dyes, so be aware of the strength of your cleaning solvent.

Rawhide can be refurbished by dusting and a light coat of neat's-foot oil. Neat's-foot oil is a common leather dressing. Use it sparingly, as too much will make the leather soft and decrease the tension in the seat.

## A WORD ABOUT RATTAN

The rattan palm is a climbing palm and often grows to great lengths using tail-like spines to grapple tree branches. It grows high, swaying among the branches of even the tallest trees. It is found in numerous locales from dense jungle areas to open forest, from sea level up to 7 or 8 thousand feet.

Like all palms the stem is solid (Figure 1-2); bamboo, with which it is often confused, is a hollow growth. There are seven genera of rattan palms, which together make up one half of the subfamily of *Lepidocaryeae* of the family *Palmae*. The most widespread genus is *Calamus*, and it along with the genus *Daemonorhops* includes the most commercially viable species. There are over two hundred known species of rattan palms, ranging over a wide area from South China and India down through the Malay Peninsula and as far distant as West Africa. The largest center of diversity, from which most of today's rattan is exported, is the Malay Peninsula, the Philippines, and Indonesia. And although about half of the species of rattans are used locally, the vast majority of rattan species has no commercial value.

Singapore and Hong Kong rattan handlers, who process huge amounts of cane, say that the best rattan comes from several districts in Indonesia and Borneo. Its color ranges from a dull red-brown to the pale yellow of *Calamus caesius*, which has long been considered the finest rattan available. It is tough and durable with long joints. Its beautifully even, unblemished surface is especially valued by furniture makers.

The stem, which is the most-used portion of the rattan palm, varies in length and thickness. Depending on the species, the thickness ranges from 3mm up to the thickness of a man's arm. There is no secondary thickening, and thus it remains a consistent size throughout its length and does not increase in thickness with age. The length varies from several yards up to two hundred yards or more. Beneath the thorny leaves is the rattan peel or outer bark. It can be smooth or ribbed and with or without the siliceous epidermis. Within the bark, at the center of the plant, is the reed core, or pith.

17

As cane is pulled from the tree tops, the newer growth is reached; here the thorny leaves are still attached. The cane leaves are twisted off by pulling the rattan around the trunk of a nearby tree. A small notch is cut in the trunk and the cane is then pulled through the notch. Friction causes the leaves and the outer bark to fall off. Sometimes cane will become firmly lodged in the tree tops, in which case a nimble member of the crew must climb the tree and cut it loose or else the quest is abandoned entirely. Rattan harvesting is generally a quite wasteful and nasty business.

When the rattan has been bundled it is brought out of the jungle to the nearest water transport. From here it is shipped down river to the warehouse to be cured. In the warehouse it is exposed to sulfur fumes overnight to kill any insects which inhabit the bark.

Rattan is sized according to diameter and graded by quality. Since the size and quality vary tremendously there are a number of categories for each. These are determined by hardness, smoothness, color, and consistency of the glossy, exterior peel. The length of the joints, or internodes, is also a factor

**1-3.** Calamus rotang, *from* Annals of the Royal Botanical Garden, *Vol. 11, by Odoardo Beccari (Calcutta, India, 1908). (Courtesy of Botanical Survey of India)*

**1-4.** Calamus siphonospathus, *from* Beccari .*(Courtesy of Botanical Survey of India)*

in grading: the best rattans are those with long joints between the leaf nodes.

Once graded the rattan is processed by passing it through a machine that strips the peel and leaves the pith exposed. Both parts go their separate ways. The cane peel is passed under a roller, where sharp knives carefully split and trim it into glossy, flat strips to be used in cane seating or wrapping. The pith, or reed core, is cut and pared lengthwise into various shapes, either dowel, square, or flat sections. The split cane and cut reed are then sold to dealers in Hong Kong or Singapore or directly to the man-ufacturers. The trimming and waste products are called crushed cane, and this is sold in bulk as packing material, matting, and a variety of other uses.

Upon arrival at the manufacturers, cane is most often woven into webbing. Large looms do most of the weaving, but they are closely attended by workers who feed strands into the design at the proper time and correct angle. Much of the so-called machine-woven cane is actually done by hand. When the webbing is finished it is rolled into bundles to await purchase by wholesalers and importers.

*1-5.* Calamus spathulatus robustus, *from* Beccari.*(Courtesy of Botanical Survey of India)*

*1-6.* Calamus scipionum, *from* Beccari.*(Courtesy of Botanical Survey of India)*

19

**1-7.** The individual weft strands are installed one at a time. (Courtesy of Cane and Basket Supply Company)

**1-8.** The diagonals are all woven by hand in the "machine woven" cane webbing. (Courtesy of Cane and Basket Supply Company)

**1-9.** At one end of the diagonal corkscrew, there is an eyelet on a swivel; at the other end the handle spins independently. The corkscrew, designed for each size mesh, is pushed rapidly through the cane, interweaving as it goes. At the other end, a strand of cane is slipped through the eyelet and the corkscrew is rapidly pulled back through the weave. (Courtesy of Cane and Basket Supply Company)

1-7.

1-9.

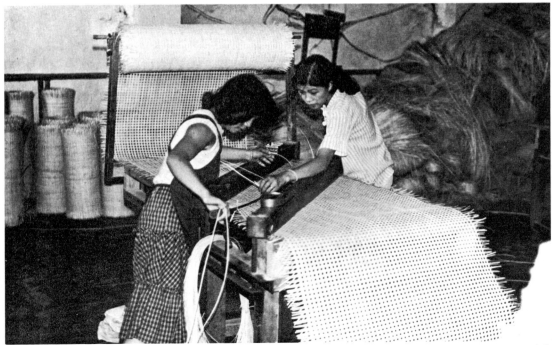

1-8.

# Machine Caning

## Restoring the Chair

Machine cane, or cane webbing as it is called commercially, is manufactured from the outer bark or peel of the rattan palm and woven on power looms. It is imported from Hong Kong, the People's Republic of China, and Indonesia, and comes in a variety of weaves (Figures 2-1 through 2-14) ranging from the traditional octagonal pattern and close-woven basket weave to the modern patterns. Since the 1950s, furniture manufacturers have custom designed cane-webbing patterns, although many were made available for only a short period of time and then discontinued.

TOOLS AND MATERIALS NEEDED

*Utility or mat knife*
*Spline chisel, ⅛ inch (3mm mortise chisel)*
*Several wooden wedges or wooden clothespins*
*Sandpaper*
*White glue*
*Wood chisel, ¾ inch (19mm)*
*Hammer*
*Machine cane*
*Spline*

The tools needed for the installing of machine cane chair seats are found in most homes, with the possible exception of the ⅛-inch narrow chisel, which is used to clear old spline from the chair seat. If you substitute this tool with something else, be careful not to damage the walls of the groove.

Spline is a wedge-shaped piece of reed from the core of the rattan palm used to anchor the machine cane in place on the chair seat. It is machined into a wedge, or V, shape that fits neatly into the groove of the chair seat. Splinelike cane webbing comes in a variety of sizes.

Machine cane can be purchased in any length up to 50 continuous feet and in widths of 12 to 24 inches (in 2-inch increments) and in widths of 30 and 36 inches for the more common patterns. The size you need depends on the chair seat to be replaced: select a piece large enough to cover the opening, with 1 inch extra on all 4 sides. Measure the caned area from front to back, groove to groove, and add 2 inches. Then measure the distance from side to side, using the groove as the measuring point, and add 2 inches. This is the size of the piece of machine cane you need. It is usually priced by the square foot.

When purchasing cane, take a sample of what you are replacing in order to match the new cane webbing to it as closely as possible. You may not be able to match the original pattern exactly, but more than likely you will find a similar pattern with a different size of cane or spacing.

You will usually need to replace the old spline (Figures 2-16 and 2-17) since it rarely comes out in one piece and is usually dam-

**2-1.** *Superfine cane in a ³⁄₈-inch open weave. The inch measurement refers to the distance between pattern repeats.*
**2-2.** *Fine-fine cane in a ⁷⁄₁₆-inch open weave.*
**2-3.** *Fine cane in a ¹⁄₂-inch open weave.*
**2-4.** *Medium cane in a ⁵⁄₈-inch open weave.*
**2-5.** *Common cane in a ³⁄₄-inch open weave.*
**2-6.** *Binder cane, 4mm wide, in a 1-inch open weave.*
**2-7.** *A ⁵⁄₈-inch open weave, with fine cane used for the warp and weft and common cane used for the diagonals.*

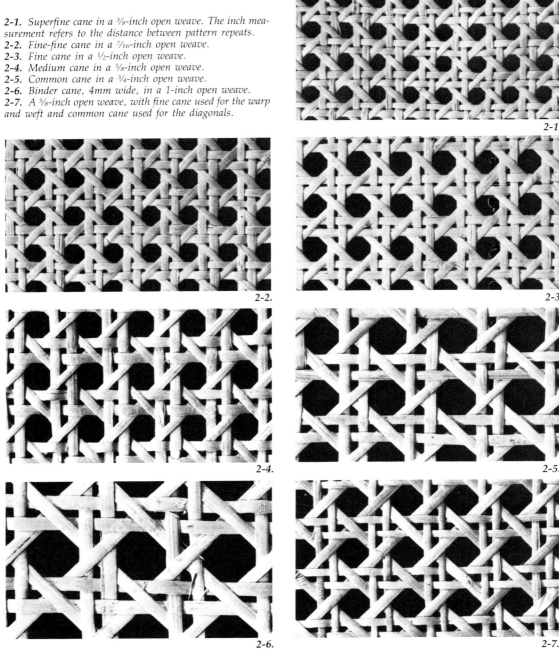

2-1.

2-2.

2-3.

2-4.

2-5.

22

2-6.

2-7.

**2-8.** *A close weave woven of medium cane (warp) and superfine cane (weft).*

**2-9.** *A close weave with common cane (warp) and medium cane (weft).*

**2-10.** *A close-woven herringbone with fine-fine cane (warp) and superfine cane (weft).*

**2-11.** *Box weave of common cane, 4 strands per inch.*

**2-12.** *Box weave of superfine cane, 7 strands per inch.*

**2-13.** *Box weave of fine-fine cane, 6 strands per inch.*

**2-14.** *Box weave of common cane, 5 strands per inch.*

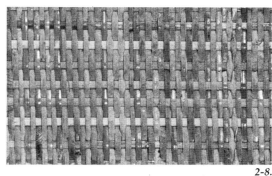

*2-8.*

*2-9.*

*2-10.*

*2-11.*

*2-12.*

*2-13.*

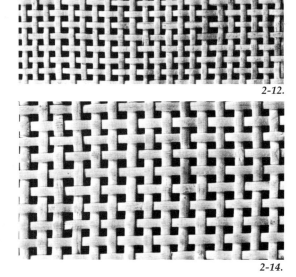

*2-14.*

23

2-15.

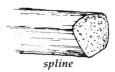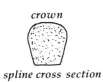

2-16.

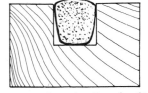

cross section of rail and spline

2-17.

spline

crown

spline cross section

**2-15.** Fifty-foot rolls of machine cane in various patterns.
**2-16.** The spline is shaped like a wedge, with a flat bottom and sides and a rounded top (called a crown).
**2-17.** The spline fits snugly into the chair's groove, with its crown flush with the seat frame, as illustrated here in cross section.

24

2-18.

2-19.

*2-18. This spline is too narrow for the groove.*
*2-19. The correct-size spline: its edges just brush the sides of the groove.*

fail for a number of reasons, one of which is having too narrow a spline.

If you cannot find the exact size spline you need, plane or "dress" down a wider piece with a small plane. A gentle sanding will also make a better fit, but most suppliers stock a wide selection of sizes and dressing down is not usually necessary.

Measure the circumference of the chair seat to determine the length of the spline needed. Add another foot to allow for cutting errors and for 4 temporary spline anchors, each about 2 inches long.

SPLINE SIZES*

| Number | Spline Size (in millimeters) | Spline Size (in inches) | Groove Size |
|---|---|---|---|
| 6½ | 2¼ × 3¾ | 3/32″ | 1/8″ |
| 7 | 3 × 5 | 7/64″ | 5/32″ |
| 7½ | 3½ × 5½ | 9/64″ | 11/64″ |
| 8 | 4 × 5½ | 5/32″ | 3/16″ |
| 8½ | 4¼ × 6 | 11/64″ | 13/64″ |
| 9 | 4¾ × 6¼ | 3/16″ | 7/32″ |
| 9½ | 5¼ × 7 | 7/32″ | 1/4″ |
| 10 | 5¾ × 7½ | 15/64″ | 9/32″ |
| 10½ | 6¼ × 8 | 1/4″ | 19/64″ |
| 11 | 6¾ × 8¾ | 17/64″ | 11/32″ |
| 12 | 7½ × 9½ | 19/64″ | 3/8″ |

*Courtesy of Cane and Basket Supply Company*

PREPARATION

Determine whether your chair is designed for cane webbing or hand caning. If the chair has many holes drilled around the seat frame, turn to Chapter Three, Hand Caning. Machine cane almost always requires a groove around the seat opening. In some cases a chair that was originally hand caned will have been grooved to make a channel suitable for machine cane. In this case there will be both holes and a groove. See Grooving

aged during removal. To determine the size of spline needed, measure the width of the chair's groove (Figures 2-18 and 2-19). The spline should be 1/32 inch smaller than the width of the groove. Measure the width of the groove at various places around the chair seat to make sure the groove is of a consistent width. For comparison when buying new spline, use a piece of old spline—providing it was the correct size originally. Seats

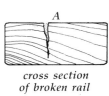

A                                    B

cross section                   cross section
of broken rail                  of repaired rail

2-20.

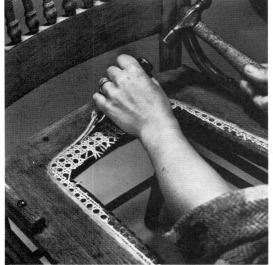

2-21.

2-22.

*2-20. A broken chair rail reinforced with glue and 1½-inch number 8 flat-head machine screw.*
*2-21. To remove the old cane webbing, cut with a mat knife along the edge of the spline to separate it from groove.*
*2-22. After you loosen the spline, remove it with a narrow, ⅛-inch (3mm) chisel.*
*2-23. Spray water into the groove to soften the old glue and make it easier to clean away.*

a Hand Caned Chair, at the end of this chapter.

Remove any tacks, nails, old cane, upholstery, leather or other materials originally used to cover the seat of your chair. If the seat was caned originally, try to determine why the seat failed so you can avoid creating the same problem. Was the groove too shallow or was too little glue used (Figure 2-20)? Has the rail broken from too much stress? Or did sharp inner edges of the seat or even a rude foot or knee do damage? If the groove was too shallow, the spline will have popped out of the groove and the cane webbing will have been pulled out and left sagging. Too much stress on the rail is apparent if the rail is weak or cracked. Figure 2-20 shows one method of shoring up a weak rail. If the sharp inner edges of the seat frame have torn the cane webbing, the tear will be at the point where the webbing meets the edge of the chair seat.

Clear away old cane with a utility or mat knife (Figure 2-21), but save a piece of it for use in choosing the new cane. Clean out the groove thoroughly (Figure 2-22). Take care in removing the old spline so as not to mar the chair. Use a spline chisel, awl, or narrow-bladed screwdriver to remove old spline. Applying water or vinegar helps loosen dirt and soften old glue that has clotted in the groove (Figure 2-23), but test vinegar on the chair's finish before using it. Also, cutting

26

2-23.

*2-24. Center the cane webbing over the chair-seat frame, with the horizontal canes parallel to the front rail. Starting in the middle of the front rail, tap the cane webbing deep into the groove with the hammer and wedge.*
*2-25. A 2-inch piece of spline anchors the webbing to the groove at the front and back rails. Pull away excess cane strands and the cotton strings woven into the selvage to make it easier to push the webbing into the groove without breaking strands.*

around the outside edge of the spline helps loosen it from the seat frame.

The groove should have vertical sides and be clean of all debris. It should be deeper than it is wide. The depth and the sides help keep the cane webbing from slipping out during installation.

Before installing the cane webbing, gently round the inside edge of the seat frame so that when the new seat is used cane will not rub against that sharp corner.

If the chair needs to be sanded or refinished, do it now—after the groove has been cleaned but before new webbing is installed. Also make any structural repairs to the chair frame now.

Soak the new cane webbing in hot (140° F = 60° C) tap water for 1 to 2 hours to insure that the cane becomes pliable. It is not necessary to soak the spline unless it seems brittle or unusually stiff. The spline will swell if it is soaked, and this makes accurate cutting of joints difficult. At most, leave spline to soak for only a few moments. Allow excess water on the cane webbing to drain before using the cane.

2-24.

2-25.

## INSTALLING THE CANE WEBBING
### Step One

Center the cane webbing, glossy side up, over the seat. Align the horizontal and vertical strands with the seat frame. Starting at the center of the front rail on the seat frame, use a blunt wooden wedge or half a wooden clothespin to push the cane into the groove (Figure 2-24). Complete about 2 inches to either side of center, and anchor the cane with a small piece of spline tapped into place.

Move to the center of the back rail, and pull the cane taut. Then repeat the procedure above, making sure the horizontal canes are parallel to the back rail. Tap a small piece of spline into the groove to anchor the webbing, as before.

Before securing cane in the side rails in a similar fashion, remove any horizontal or vertical cane strands that fall at or beyond the groove outside the exposed seat area; do this by pulling them free of their mesh (Figure 2-25). You will also have to remove the cotton string woven into the selvage. By removing excess strands, you reduce tension on the strands being tapped into the groove, allowing them to conform to their new shape without breaking at the edge.

Now go to the side rails. Tap the cane into about 2 inches of groove, anchor the webbing with a short piece of spline, pull the cane taut, and anchor it on the opposite side rail (Figure 2-26). The cane is now held at

2-26.

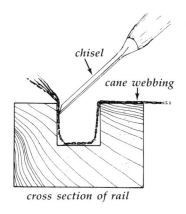

2-29.

2-27.

2-28.

2-26. *The cane webbing has been anchored at all 4 rails.*
2-27. *Remove the diagonal strands that are outside the finished seat area.*
2-28. *Working toward the corners, push the cane webbing into the groove.*
2-29. *With a chisel, trim excess can just below the outside edge of the groove, shown here in cross section without the spline in place.*

4 points, with horizontal strands parallel to the front and back chair rails and vertical strands oriented to the side chair rails.

Remove any diagonal strands that are outside the seat area (Figure 2-27). Carefully pull them along their axis so as not to distort the symmetry of the other strands.

Working toward the corners, tap the rest of the cane webbing deep into the groove (Figure 2-28). The cane should become taut and smooth, lying flat against the top of the seat frame with equal tension all around.

**Step Two**

With a sharp wood chisel, trim the edge of the cane webbing just below the outside edge of the groove (Figure 2-29). Alternatively, a mat knife can be used (Figures 2-30 and 2-31), but be careful not to pull the cane out of the groove. You may need to remove the temporary spline anchors to accomplish this. Work slowly to avoid damaging the wood chair frame.

Generously pour glue into the groove on top of the trimmed cane webbing (Figure 2-32). Any excess that is forced out when the spline is inserted can be wiped up later. If too little glue is used, the spline is likely to one day pop out.

2-30.

2-31.

2-32.

2-33.

*2-30. When using a chisel to trim the cane, be careful not to damage the adjacent wood.*
*2-31. You can also use a mat knife to trim the excess cane, but be careful not to pull the cane out of the groove.*
*2-32. Generously pour glue into the groove.*
*2-33. Starting at the middle of the back rail, tap the spline into the groove. Use a block of wood to protect the spline's crown.*

**Step Three**

With a hammer and block of wood, set the spline into the groove. Start in the middle of the back rail with one end of the spline, tapping it gently into the groove all the way around the chair seat (Figure 2-33). Use the wedge and hammer in conjunction, as using just the hammer will damage the crown of the spline. Tap the spline down into the groove until its crown is flush with the seat frame, and wipe away any excess glue that seeps out.

If the corners of the groove are rounded or if the chair seat is round, the spline can run the entire circumference in one piece. The use of one continuous piece of spline will result in a butt joint in the middle of the back rail. If the corners of the groove are square or sharp you will need to use several pieces of spline. The excess spline should be marked and cut with a sharp mat knife or pruning shears (Figure 2-34).

When using several pieces of spline in a square or angular seat frame, mitred ends or ends cut at an angle produce a neater join than do ends (Figure 2-36) cut straight and simply butted at the corners.

29

2-34.

2-35.

2-36.

*2-34. Cut the spline with a mat knife or pruning shears.*
*2-35. The finished seat, with the spline tapped into place flush with the seat frame.*
*2-36. A machine-caned seat with mitered spline corners.*

Let the newly caned seat be for 24 hours, allowing the glue to set and the webbing (Figure 2-35) to dry. As the cane dries it will shrink; tension will increase and make a smooth, taut seat. The more slowly the cane dries, the tighter it will become.

FINISHING

Once the cane is dry you can color it with a varnish stain or let it tan naturally with age. Leave the underside of the cane webbing free of stain and sealer so that moisture and oil can penetrate. Oil the cane once or twice a year to keep it from drying out and becoming brittle although this is generally not necessary for the first several years. Lemon oil, Danish furniture oil, or a mixture of 1 part boiled linseed oil and 2 parts paint thinner will do. (Do not attempt to boil linseed oil yourself.) Be sure to wipe away the excess oil after 15 minutes.

If the seat begins to sag with heavy use, tighten it by sponging the cane with hot water and allowing it to dry slowly. This should bring it back to its original tension.

**Special Techniques**

There are quite a few variations of the groove-and-spline method of installing cane webbing, some of which are detailed below.

INSTALLING A MEDALLION

Some wing-back chairs, couches, and large armchairs have medallions locked into the center of an area of cane webbing. The method for installing these often ornate medallions is similar to the regular groove-and-spline method of caning. The difference is that the medallion is installed into the webbing instead of vice versa.

Position the medallion on the installed cane webbing and lightly mark its placement (Figure 2-37). Cut a hole in the webbing 2 inches smaller in diameter than the diameter of the medallion. Place the medallion behind the cane and push the cane webbing

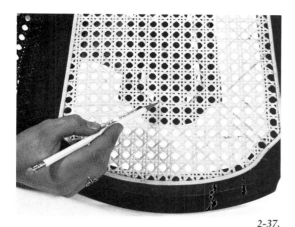

2-37.

2-38.

2-37. *Lightly mark the cane webbing where the medallion will be placed.*
2-38. *Place the medallion behind the cane and push the can· into the medallion's groove as you would in a chair seat.*
2-39. *The finished chair, with medallion in place at the center of the chair back.*

into the medallion's groove. Anchor it with small pieces of spline on opposite sides (Figure 2-38). You may have to place a block of wood behind the medallion to bring it to the correct level. Remove the small pieces of spline and trim the excess cane just below the inside edge of the medallion's groove.

Pour white glue into the groove on top of the trimmed cane. Tap in the spline with a hammer and a block of wood. Cut the spline to form a neat butt joint and let the glue set for 24 hours (Figure 2-39).

## GROOVING A HAND-CANED SEAT FOR MACHINE CANE

It is our opinion that a hand-caned seat should be restored by hand caning. However, if you want a functional chair and do not want to hand cane the seat, then you can channel a groove in the seat frame for machine cane. It is a simple process. A hand-held electric drill is used to rout the groove, and other tools such as a router or hand chisel may be used with slight variations.

2-39.

31

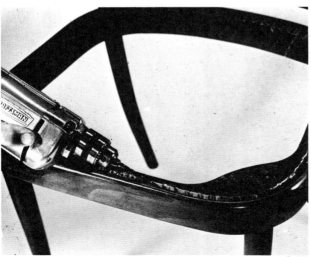

2-40. *To create a groove in a chair that was originally hand caned, drill new holes between the original holes. Drill only partially into—not through—the rail.*

2-41. *Use a hand-held electric drill to connect the holes, forming a groove or channel in the seat frame.*

Mark around the seat frame (the wood should be at least ¾-inch thick) with a pencil and ruler to indicate where the groove will be. The holes already drilled in the seat frame for the hand-caned seat are your guide; they should lie at least ¾ inch from the opening of the frame. The groove should not be any wider than these holes—preferably ³⁄₁₆ inch to ¼ inch. With a hammer and center punch, mark holes to be drilled between and to connect the existing holes. These additional holes are drilled only as deep as the groove will be, and are drilled solely for the purpose of removing the excess wood between existing holes. Using a hand-held electric drill (Figure 2-40), keep the line straight and drill no deeper than necessary; the rail already has a number of holes to weaken it. The groove should be 25 to 50 percent deeper than it is wide, and its sides should be vertical and square at the bottom. The hand-held electric drill (Figure 2-41) is sufficient for the initial work. Use a wood chisel to finish the groove.

When the groove is made, check the rails for strength. A weakened rail will show cracks along the line of the new groove. Countersink several screws to shore up a weakened rail.

Before installing the cane, place masking tape around the bottom of the seat frame to cover the original holes in the rail so that the glue does not drip through. When the seat is completed and the glue is dry, remove the masking tape.

2-40.

2-41.

*2-42. A finished chair, with its original hand-caned back and the newly installed prewoven machine-cane seat.*
*2-43. Four wood supports are removed from the chair frame before securing the cane webbing.*

### Three Variations

While a groove-and-reed spline became the common means of securing machine caning, another method was also utilized when machine-woven cane became available in the early 1870s.

Four pieces of wood screwed to the inside of the chair frame (Figure 2-43) or in the case of a round seat, a single bent piece of wood screwed to the inside of the chair frame, sandwiches the cane webbing in place.

To install the new cane webbing, unscrew and remove the inner support frame from the chair. Then clear away any old cane remnants still clinging to the frame or support pieces. From underneath, insert the new piece of cane webbing (with at least 2 inches of overlap), and sandwich the wooden support by hand to the front rail. Apply pressure. When you have decided that the cane is running parallel to the front rail and is centered properly in the opening, screw the front support piece to the inside of the front rail. Pull the cane to the back of the seat and hand hold it in place with the back support piece. Make sure that all the cut cane edges are toward the bottom of the seat. Tug individual strands down as necessary before tightly screwing the back rail support in place. Ease the side pieces in place from the underside of the seat, making sure the cane edges are all sandwiched properly. You will probably have to loosen the front and back supports and readjust some of the cane strands as you attach the side supports. When the cane is centered and aligned, tighten all the screws completely (Figure 2-44). Trim the cane with a mat knife where

2-42.

2-43.

2-44.

2-45.

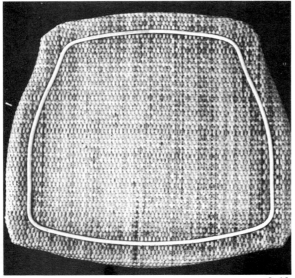

34

2-46.

**2-44.** *After securing the cane webbing to the front and back rails, the side supports are screwed into place.*

**2-45.** *A continuous wooden rim sandwiches the prewoven cane into place by being screwed into the inside of this rocker's seat frame.*

**2-46.** *An unusual seat found on Chinese Chippendale-style chairs. The close-woven webbing is set into the groove without cutting and is held in place with spline. It is then wrapped around to the underside of the seat frame, where it is wedged into another groove on the bottom of the chair. Because the cane webbing would bunch at the corners, there is a small cut in each corner and the strands are individually woven to make a tight, neat edge.*

the cane emerges on the underside of the seat. No glue is necessary in this application.

Another variant calls for the groove to be on the underside of the seat frame. The webbing is pulled around the edges of the seat and attached on the underside, and some hand splicing is necessary at the corners to interweave individual strands of the webbing so that they will neatly cover the corners of the seat. Remove several strands near the corner where the webbing bunches. The interweaving of the loose strands should approximate the pattern on the rest of the webbing (Figure 2-46).

A third variation is found on some modern door panels where cane is stapled into a rabbet (an L-shaped joint) and sandwiched in place by a piece of wooden molding.

# Hand Caning:
# The Seven Step Method

The Seven Step method is the predominant pattern used in hand caning, and most professional and amateur craftspeople would agree that it is one of the best. It forms a strong yet flexible seat that will last many years.

If your chair has a series of holes running lengthwise up each rail, then it should be restored by hand caning. If the chair is round and the holes in the rails run the circumference of the seat frame, turn to Chapter 4, Special Techniques in Hand Caning, and follow the instructions for caning chairs with curved rails.

The Seven Step method is suitable for almost all chairs that need hand caning. In most chairs the holes in the rails are regularly spaced and evenly drilled. Occasionally, however, a chair will have odd-size holes or a different number of holes on opposing rails. This problem is most commonly found on handmade or country furniture. In all cases, including these irregular chairs mentioned above, try to follow the Seven-Step method as closely as possible. There will inevitably be variations between chairs, and the caner must adapt to each.

## Restoring the Chair

The chair used as an example for the Seven Step method is a factory-made Victorian exemplary of a wide variety of hand-caned chairs in that its size, the number of holes, and its basic style are common.

TOOLS AND MATERIALS NEEDED

*Wood rasp*
*Utility or mat knife*
*Tack hammer*
*Clothespin*
*Wooden or reed pegs*
*Tape measure or ruler*
*Ice pick*
*Needlenose pliers*
*Small hand clippers or shears*
*Bucket or tub*
*Sponge*
*Tack rag*
*Cane, 250 feet*
*Binder cane, 15 feet*

No *special* tools are needed for caning, since each is commonly found in the home. Some substitutions can be made, such as rubber bands, large paper clips, or string for clothespins, and an awl in place of the ice pick. You will need about a dozen pegs, which can be made by sharpening 1½-inch lengths of spline or round reed with a pencil sharpener. Some caners whittle maple dowels into pegs, while others have found a new use for golf tees.

Cane comes in hanks of 1000 feet. Each hank consists of many pieces varying in length from 10 to 20 feet. This amount is sufficient to cover 4 ordinary chairs each approximately 12 inches by 12 inches, or having 72 holes. Mail-order houses or supply

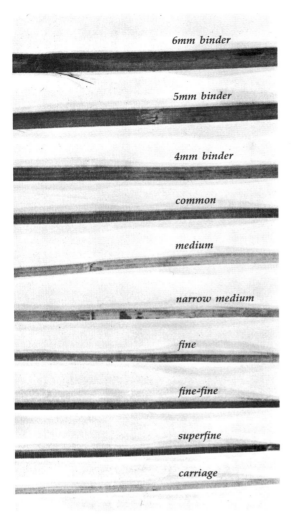

6mm binder

5mm binder

4mm binder

common

medium

narrow medium

fine

fine-fine

superfine

carriage

**3-1.**

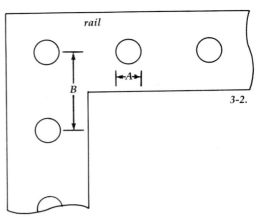

rail

B

A

**3-2.**

**3-1.** Sizes of canes commonly available.
**3-2.** To find the correct size of the cane required for your chair, measure the diameter of the hole (A), and the distance between the centers of 2 adjacent holes (B), on the side rail.

6 times through each hole. To determine the size of cane needed for your chair, consult the chart below. The strongest consideration should be the distance between holes (Figure 3-2).

CHOOSING A CANE SIZE

| Size | Cane width (*in millimeters*) | Diameter of hole (*in inches*) | Distance between holes (*in inches*) |
|---|---|---|---|
| Common | 3.5 | 5/16 | 7/8 |
| Medium | 3 | 1/4 | 3/4 |
| Narrow Medium | 2.75 | 1/4 | 11/16 |
| Fine | 2.5 | 7/32 | 5/8 |
| Fine-fine | 2-2.5 | 3/16 | 1/2 |
| Superfine | 1.75 | 1/8 | 3/8 |
| Carriage | 1.5 | 1/8 | 3/8 |

Binder cane differs from other cane only in that it is traditionally 1 or 2 sizes larger than the cane used in the weaving. It is 4 to 6mm, and is the accepted term for the 3 sizes of cane larger than "common."

Because cane is a natural fiber it varies in quality, so try to select the best—long, glossy strips—when purchasing it. Cane lengths generally vary between 10 and 20 feet. Shorter lengths require more tying off, while longer lengths require more time in weaving the excess length; you'll have to decide which you prefer.

houses often sell cane in half hanks of 500 feet or quarter hanks of 250 feet. Cane, always measured in millimeters, comes in various sizes (Figure 3-1). It is very important that you take careful measurements and buy and use the correct size cane. At several different places on the chair, measure the width or diameter of each hole; then measure the distance between holes, from the center of one hole to the center of the next (Figure 3-2). The distance between the holes determines the spacing of the woven pattern and therefore the size of cane to use. (If spacing is uneven, use the average distance between holes in 6 inches.) The diameter of the hole itself does not determine the cane size and is measured only as an added gauge to the correct size. Remember the smaller the hole the smaller the cane size, because the cane strand may pass as many as 4 to

*tail end: peg this end in chair*  *leaf node*

*younger growth*  *weave with this end*

**3-3.** *Cane strand showing leaf node, or eye, and weaving end.*

Select cane that is uniform in color, tough yet pliable, smooth and glossy on the top-side, and smoothly edged. Poor-quality cane has rough spots and black or brown discoloring, and may be very thin and have linear splits. It will take longer to weave because it will break or split easily as it is handled and woven. All cane, even that of good quality, has small bumps every 18 to 24 inches; these slightly rough bumps are nodes, where the palm leaf was attached (Figure 3-3).

Always store cane in a cool, slightly moist place to prevent its drying out. If the cane has been stored or shipped in a coil, straighten it (which is quite easy) by soaking it in warm water very briefly and then hanging it out loosely to dry. Its own weight will tend to dry it straight, making it ready to use.

PREPARATION

Before removing old cane from a chair, take a good look at its size and the pattern of its weave. Make a written or mental note on which holes the diagonal steps have skipped or doubled up. The diagonal steps, the fifth and sixth steps of the Seven-Step method, are the strands that run diagonally across the seat as you face the chair. In some cases a chair may have been caned poorly in the first place, so to copy a poor job would be of little use. To determine whether a chair has been caned improperly, ask yourself: Is it pleasing? are the holes in the cane pattern evenly spaced? do the diagonal strands run smoothly across the seat? Run your eye along the edge of the seat along the binder cane. Do the cane strands form a series of x's and fisheyes? A fisheye occurs when 2 diagonal strands double up in the same hole. If you can answer yes to these questions, the chair has been caned well. And if a few simple rules are followed, anyone can achieve the same good results.

To remove all the old cane, use a mat knife to cut the center out of the old cane seat. Then use an ice pick and clippers to clean out the holes. Sometimes glue and dirt clog the holes; clean this away with a hand-held electric drill. Pull out any nails or tacks. Clear away upholstery, leather, or other material that may have been attached to the chair. Go over the chair with tack cloth moistened with paint thinner to clean away any dirt or grease. Use a wood rasp to gently round the top inside edge of the seat frame; a sharp edge might tear the new seat.

Make necessary structural repairs to the chair at this time. Remember that the new cane seat will exert considerable pressure on the seat frame, possibly making any existing

**3-4.** *This is a Victorian factory-made chair ready for caning.*

**3-4.**

small cracks worse. Refinish the chair if it is needed or desired.

Before starting to weave, coil a number of strands of cane and individually clip them with a clothespin. Place them in a bucket or tub of warm (100° to 140° F, 38° to 60° C) for 15 minutes to make them elastic and pliable. Throughout the weaving only, keep the cane wet. When you are not working on the seat, you can let the cane dry out; but when you come back to work, sponge the seat down with warm water. Some caners prefer to add glycerine or urea crystals to the water. This really isn't necessary if warm water is used, unless the cane is exceptionally old and brittle. Adding glycerine or urea crystals might make the weaving a little easier, but a seat woven of old and brittle materials will not last very long anyway.

WEAVING THE SEAT

**Step One**

Find the middle of the front and back rails. To do so, first count the number of holes in the back rail of the seat frame. If there is an odd number of holes, determine the center hole and put a peg in it for reference. If there is an even number of holes in the back rail, place a peg in the hole to the right of where the center hole would have been (Figure 3-5). Use the same method to determine the center hole in the front rail.

Now determine the "tail" end of the cane. Look closely at the glossy side and find where the leaf was attached. This will be marked by a ¼-inch-long bump or an uneven spot in the cane surface every 18 to 24 inches. Examine this bump and find the side that is slightly lower than the other. The lower side is where the new cane grew from the older stem. Run your fingernail across this joint; in one direction it will catch and in the other direction it will traverse smoothly. The direction in which your nail can run

smoothly is the direction in which you want to weave. *When caning, you always want the cane to traverse smoothly.*

Remove the peg in the back rail and insert 4 inches of the tail end of the cane into the hole. Replace the peg to secure the cane in the hole.

Pull the strand of cane, glossy side up, across to the front rail. Remove the peg from the center hole and insert the cane. Pull the cane through until it is taut between the 2 holes (Figure 3-6), then replace the peg to secure the cane. It is not necessary to leave any slack.

Bring the cane up through the next hole to the right on the front rail. Hold the loop on the underside of the chair frame tight; it should not be twisted, and the glossy side should be facing outward (Figure 3-7). By holding the loop tight against the underside of the rail with your forefinger, you can move the peg on the topside of the front rail to the next hole to secure the cane. This peg will be used alternately between the front and back rails to secure the cane strand as it passes through successive holes until the strand is too short to weave.

Return the cane strand to the back rail (Figures 3-8 and 3-9) and into the hole directly to the right of the first peg. Pull the cane up through the next hole to the right on the back rail. On the underside of the rail, hold the loop tight with a finger while you secure the cane with a peg.

Continue working to the right, weaving the cane back and forth between the front and back rails. Keep the glossy side of the cane up and the loops tight and untwisted. If the cane ends before the right side is finished, leave it pegged and start a new strand at the adjacent hole.

On most chairs, the front rail will be wider than the back rail. Because of this, the strand coming from the front rail will probably end in a hole along the side rail. At this stage,

3-5.

3-5. There is an even number of holes on the front and back of this chair. Because there are no holes in the exact center of the rails, the pegs are placed in the first hole to the right of where the center hole would have been. Note that the pegs are opposite each other.

3-6. Peg four inches of the cane into the back rail, glossy side up, then bring the cane strand across to the equivalent hole in the front rail.

3-7. The cane has been pulled taut between the front and back rails and secured with a peg. It is then brought up through the adjacent hole to the right on the front rail while a finger holds the loop secure on the underside.

3-8. Step One.

3-9. Secure the cane with a peg in the front rail while you bring it to the back rail.

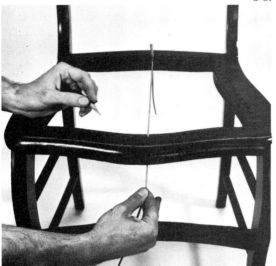

3-6.

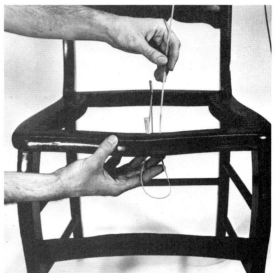

3-7.

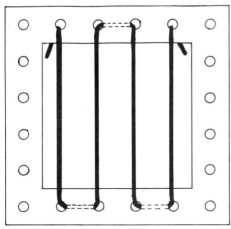

3-8.

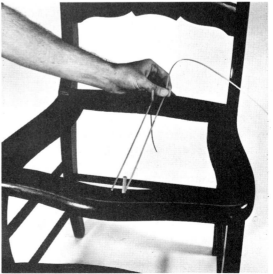

3-9.

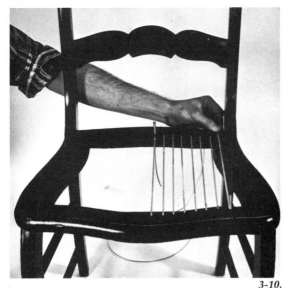

3-10.

3-11.

3-12.

3-13.

**3-10.** *Do not bring the cane through the back right-hand corner hole. Leave the corner hole free.*

**3-11.** *Peg the end of the cane in the right-hand rail, parallel to the preceding strands, so that it does not cover any holes on the rail.*

**3-12.** *To complete the left side, peg a new strand in the back rail in the first hole to the left of the starting hole. Bring the cane across to the equivalent hole on the front rail.*

**3-13.** *Since the front rail is longer than the back rail on most chair seats, short fill-in strands from the front rail to the side rail are often needed. The rule is to keep the strands parallel and not to cover any holes on the side rail.*

do not use the back corner hole (Figure 3-10). Peg the cane in a hole in the side rail (Figure 3-11), leaving the corner hole free for later steps, specifically the diagonal strands. To determine which hole on the side rail to use, follow these standards: (1) The strand should be pegged so that it is parallel with the previous strands. (2) The strand should not be pegged in a hole where it will cover other holes in the side rail.

To weave the left side of the chair, start by pegging a new strand of cane in the hole directly to the left of the hole in which the weaving started. Bring the cane across and into the equivalent hole on the front rail (Figure 3-12). Continue in this fashion, completing the left side in the same manner as

3-14.

3-14. To begin Step Two, peg the cane into the first hole after the corner hole at the back of the left-hand rail.
3-15. Step Two.
3-16: Step Two is complete, but there is too much space along the front rail. A fill-in strand is needed here.

you did the right side; both halves should be identical when finished.

To finish Step One, you will often need to fill the space at the front corners of the chair with one or more short pieces of cane (Figure 3-13). The number of fill-in strands needed is determined by the number of vacant holes on the front rail, excluding the corner holes. Cut a short length of cane, about 12 to 18 inches. Peg it into the vacant hole on the front rail. Bring the strand to the side rail so that it is parallel to the other strands. Peg it into the appropriate hole on the side rail. In this manner, continue filling all but the corner holes on the front rail.

**Step Two**

Peg a new strand of cane in the first rear hole of the left-hand rail. Do not use the corner hole. Bring the cane over and across Step One strands and through the equivalent hole on the right-hand rail (Figure 3-14). This will be the hole in front of and directly next to the corner hole. Secure the cane with a peg. Pull the cane strand up through the next hole on the right-hand rail, bring it back across the left-hand rail, and pull it through the next hole (Figure 3-15). Continue this side-to-side weave until you reach the front rail. If some holes on the side rail already have pegs in them from Step One, remove each peg, pass the new strand through the new hole, and replace the peg.

Generally, as with the chair in Figure 3-16, you will need a fill-in strand along the front rail. Sometimes you will also need a fill-in strand along the back rail. (Fill-in

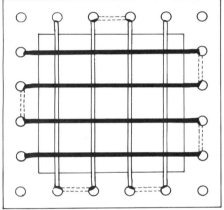

3-15.

3-16.

41

3-17.

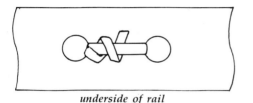

underside of rail

3-18.

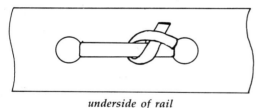

underside of rail

3-19.

*3-17. This fill-in strand, like earlier ones, is parallel to the other strands and does not cover any other holes.*
*3-18. In this method of tying off, bring the loose cane end under the loop twice to secure it.*
*3-19. Another way to tie off is to tuck the loose cane under the loop and then under itself to form a secure overhand knot.*

warm water by running a sponge over each one. This increases the elasticity of the cane, making it easier to manipulate. There are 2 methods, or knots, used for tying off; both are quite simple. In the first (Figure 3-18), you gently lift the loop next to a free end by inserting the ice pick under it. It should give slightly. Tuck the loose strand under the loop and pull it taut. Bring the end over the loop and then under it again, pulling it taut. When the cane dries, this knot will be secure.

With the second method (Figure 3-19), gently lift the loop with the ice pick, as before. Tuck the end under the loop but don't pull it taut yet. Bring the end back over the loop and under itself. Pull the knot tight. This knot, called an overhand knot, is adequate for securing the cane but makes the underside of the seat bulkier.

**Step Three**

This step (Figure 3-20) is similar to Step One, with two slight variations. First, the cane strand is started on the front rail rather than on the back as in Step One. This is to create more loops on the underside of the chair, making it easier for you to tie off more loose cane ends.

Second, the strands rest on top of the cane previously woven (Figure 3-21); however, each strand is pegged lying slightly to the right of those woven in Step One (Figure 3-22). Though emerging from the same hole, the strands of Steps One and Three are both visible. This makes Step Four much easier to weave.

To weave Step Three, peg a new strand of cane in the center hole in the front rail, leaving, as always, about 4 inches of cane hanging free on the underside of the chair frame. Peg the cane on the right-hand side of the hole so that the strand lies just to the right of the strand woven in Step One. Use the ice pick to adjust the strand as needed.

strands are most common on chairs with bowed rails.) Stretch a short piece of cane between 2 holes on the front rail to approximate the parallel pattern already achieved (Figure 3-17). Peg both ends.

Turn the chair over and, with clippers, cut off the excess cane strands, leaving about 4 inches hanging free. These end pieces are used to tie off the cane strands so that the pegs can be removed.

(Only free ends that have a loop coming out of the same hole are tied off at this stage. If there are no adjacent loops, leave the peg in the hole and go on to the next step. There will be plenty of opportunity later for tying off these ends.)

First, wet the loops and the cane ends with

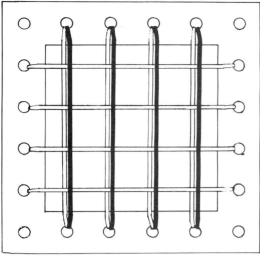

3-20.

**3-20.** *Step Three.*

**3-21.** *In Step Three, lay the cane over previously woven cane. Start the cane strand in the front rail which will create more loops on the underside.*

**3-22.** *The weaving here follows Step One. The cane strands occupy the same holes as the strands woven in Step One, but they are laid consistently to the right of the earlier strands.*

**3-23.** *Step Three is now complete. All strands are slightly to the right of previous ones to aid in the weaving of Step Four. This includes the fill-in strands along the side rails.*

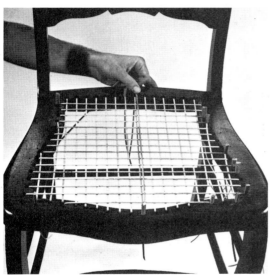

3-21.

3-23.

3-22.

Bring the cane across to the back rail and down through the center hole. Now bring the strand up through the next hole to the right and then pull the cane back to the front rail.

Continue laying the cane following Step One. The strands should finish in the holes on the side rail used in Step One.

To weave the left half of the chair, peg a new strand of cane in the front rail in the hole to the left of where Step Three began. Bring the cane to the back rail, and so on. Remember, even though the weave is moving to the left, the strands must be laid consistently to the right of those woven in Step One (Figure 3-23).

43

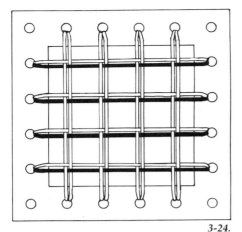

3-24.

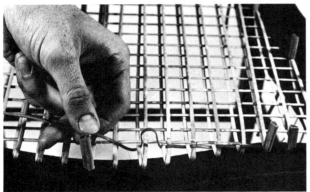

3-25.

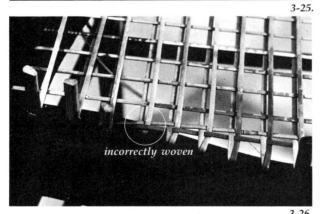

*incorrectly woven*

3-26.

*correctly woven*

44

3-27.

*3-24. Step Four.*
*3-25. Begin Step Four by weaving the fill-in piece on the front rail. Weave the cane over Step Three strands under those of Step One, and in front of Step Two.*
*3-26. An incorrect ending! Always weave all the way across to the hole, never overlap a pair of strands.*
*3-27. A correct ending! The cane weaves through every pair to the hole.*

**Step Four**

This is the first actual weaving step; that is, it is at this point that the cane strand is interwoven, over and under other strands.

Two things are crucial here. First, the tail end of the cane must always be pegged to facilitate weaving. Second, all strands, including the ones already woven, should be kept wet and elastic throughout the weaving. If only the weaving strand is kept wet, it will ripple while the others lie flat. This ripple is caused by the stiffness of the dry strands.

The weaving of Step Four is from side to side. Weave the strands so that they lie in front of the strands woven in Step Two. When you are moving left to right, weave under the strands of Step One and over the strands of Step Three. When you are moving from right to left, weave over Step Three strands and under Step One.

Start at the front rail and weave the fill-in strand first (Figure 3-25). (It is much easier to weave this now than later, when the tension of the weave will have dramatically increased.) Then peg a new short strand on the left-hand side of the front rail in the same hole that the fill-in strand of Step Two begins. Weave this new strand so that it lies beside and in front of the Step Two fill-in strand. Always weave across to a hole (Figures 3-26 and 3-27). Use an ice pick to aid in weaving where the strands are tight or against the rail.

Select a new strand of generous length, and peg it into the right-hand rail in the hole in front of the back corner hole. By starting on this side, the loops on the underside will alternate with the loops created in Step Two. Keep the glossy side of the cane up, and avoid twists. Weave, with the tip of the cane, about one-third of the way across; then pull the cane taut. Give an extra tug to equalize the ripple in all the strands, and then con-

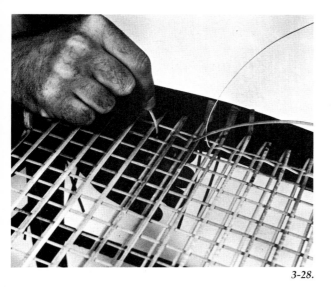

3-28.

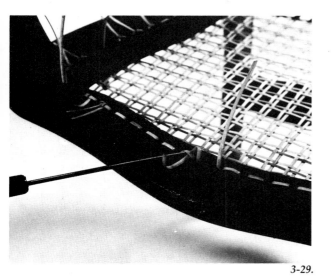

3-29.

*3-28.* One hand is on the bottom and one on the top. The hand below returns the cane end to the topside by pushing it up through the adjacent hole.
*3-29.* When Step Four is finished, turn the chair over and tie off the loose ends.
*3-30.* A good method of straightening the weave. Place an ice pick against the strands and gently tap on the side with a tack hammer.

Wet the loops and any free cane ends. Tie off the ends as described in Step Two (Figure 3-29). Try not to tie more than 2 knots on each loop. Any loose strands not adjacent to a loop can be left for later.

Before moving on to Steps Five and Six, straighten the cane pattern. The object is to make the pattern appear as close to a grid as possible, with pairs of strands uniformly spaced both horizontally and vertically. Bring the strands close together in pairs and into straight lines between their holes. The best way to do this is with an ice pick or awl and a tack hammer together. Using your fingers will only make them more sore than they already are.

Place the ice pick perpendicular to and against dampened cane (Figure 3-30). Tap the side of the ice pick with the tack hammer, which will gently maneuver the strand into alignment. Start on a middle strand, straightening the cane along an imaginary line between 2 holes. Use each successive strand as a guide for the next, aligning each with its respective holes.

tinue to weave another third of the way across.

Place one hand underneath the seat and one hand on top. The hand below returns the cane to the topside by pushing it up through the adjacent hole (Figure 3-28). Weave through several strands before taking up the slack. Working approximately a third of the way across the seat at a time is sufficient to let the strand pull through easily. By weaving farther than this, the tension on the strand becomes too great and it will break.

Continue weaving from side to side, a third of the way at a time. As Step Four nears completion, the tension in the weave will increase with the addition of each new woven strand.

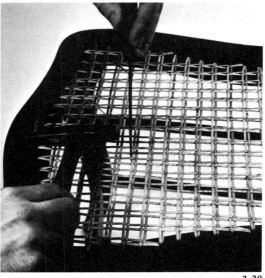

3-30.

45

3-31.

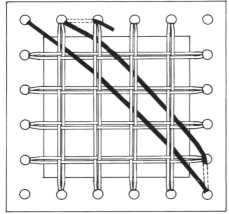

3-32.

3-33.

*3-31. An alternate method of straightening the weave. Hold a reed peg in each hand, and push and squeeze the cane into position.*
*3-32. Step Five.*
*3-33. Start Step Five at the back left-hand corner hole. Bring the tip of the cane under the strands of Steps One and Three and over those of Steps Two and Four, in a stair-step fashion.*

An alternative method of aligning the cane strands is to take 2 reed pegs—one in each hand—and to push and squeeze the cane into place (Figure 3-31).

### Step Five

Of all the steps, the diagonals require the most planning. You must always be 2 steps ahead of yourself. Examine figures 3-32 to 3-38 to acquaint yourself with this step before starting. Although many chairs may look quite similar, they are almost always somewhat different when it comes down to particulars. It is not the weaving of the diagonal that is difficult, but the selecting of the correct holes with which to end them that is elusive; some holes along the side and front rails will be skipped, while others might have double strands of cane or fisheyes.

Always weave the diagonal strand in a stair-step pattern and weave as far as you can, going over and under as many horizontal and vertical strands as possible. The stair-step pattern looks just like a staircase—up, then over, then repeating the same motion again. The diagonal strands will not always go in a perfectly straight line to a hole but may veer or curve to it.

Peg a strand in the back left-hand corner hole. Weave under the strands of Steps One and Three and over those of Steps Two and Four (Figure 3-33). The same instructions could also read "under the verticals (front to back) and over the horizontals (side to side)." If the weave is done correctly, the cane strand will pull through easily.

For the first diagonal, weave the cane one-third of the way across the seat at a time. It will end in the opposite corner hole only if you have a perfectly square seat or if there is the same number of holes on each rail. At the opposite side, the strand can move to either the right or the left of the hole the cane has just entered. Choose a hole that will allow you to bring the cane strand back

*3-34. The cane has traversed the chair diagonally and has returned to the starting corner to form a "fisheye."*

*3-35. The starting strand for the front half of Step Five. Notice that on this chair the fifth and tenth holes above the right corner hole are skipped to keep the pattern of the diagonals in parallel alignment.*

*3-36. An example of how not to weave the diagonals. The strand here is out of line toward the center of the front rail. The diagonal should have been doubled in the fifth hole from the right.*

*3-37. Here the diagonal is correctly doubled in the fifth hole from the right. Always go under, over, under as far as possible. Your diagonal will not necessarily be doubled in the fifth hole, but keep in mind the stair step motion if you see your diagonals being pulled out of line.*

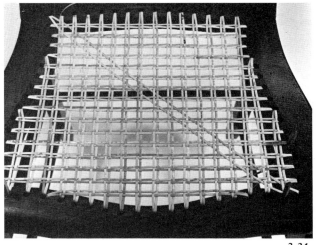

3-34.

to the starting corner hole. Find the correct hole, bring the cane up through it, and weave across to the starting corner hole, doubling up to make a "fisheye" (Figure 3-34).

Once the strand is back at the starting corner hole, bring it next to the right. Continue weaving diagonals across, always weaving under the verticals and over the horizontals. The last diagonal usually finishes in the 2 holes adjacent to the back right-hand corner hole. If the front rail has more holes than the back rail, fill-in strands will be in place on the right rail. The diagonals skip the first hole to the front of the fill-in strand on the right rail.

To finish the front half of the chair, start a new strand of cane and weave the diagonals toward the front corner (Figure 3-35). Two diagonal strands will enter the same hole on the left-hand rail, one hole in front of the hole that the fill-in strand occupies. This doubling, or fisheye, occurs with each fill-in strand.

If you choose an inappropriate hole in which to end a diagonal, pull the strand out and start again (Figures 3-36 and 3-37). *A*

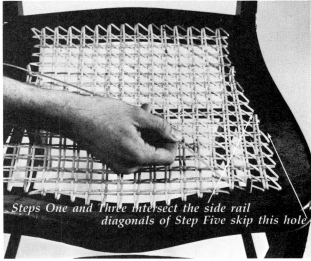

*Steps One and Three intersect the side rail diagonals of Step Five skip this hole*

3-35.

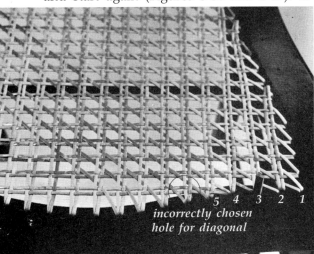

5 4 3 2 1
*incorrectly chosen hole for diagonal*

3-36.

5 4 3 2 1

3-37.

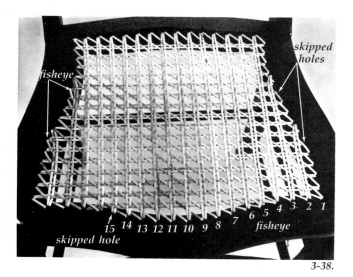

3-38.

*3-38. Step Five is complete. Two holes on the right-hand rail were skipped, and 2 holes on the left hand rail have double diagonal strands. Along the front rail, the fifth hole is doubled and the fifteenth hole is skipped.*

*3-39. Step Six.*

*3-40. Begin Step Six at the back right-hand corner. In a stair-step pattern, weave under the strands of Steps Two and Four and over those of Steps One and Three.*

mistake will compound itself with each successive diagonal woven, eventually throwing the whole pattern into imbalance (Figure 3-36).

Check your progress by imagining the horizontal and vertical strands as a stairway, and weave over and under until there are no more stairs to ascend or descend (Figure 3-38).

### Step Six

Step Six, the second diagonal, is a mirror image of the first diagonal (Figure 3-39). Where a hole was skipped on the right-hand rail in Step Five, a hole will be skipped in the left-hand rail in Step Six. Where a fisheye was made on the left-hand rail, a fisheye will now be made on the right-hand rail.

Peg a new strand in the back right-hand corner hole (Figure 3-40). Weave under the strands of Steps Two and Four and over those of Steps One and Three. The instructions could also read "under the horizontals and over the verticals." Step Six strands run perpendicular to those of Step Five and move over, under, and over each successive diagonal strand. Be sure to cross the last diagonal before inserting the strand in a hole. Never cross over 2 diagonal strands in succession.

Weave directly across to the opposite side, passing the cane through the appropriate hole. Bring the cane up through an adjacent hole on either the right or left side (Figure 3-41). As before, use whichever hole will allow you to end in the starting corner hole to make the fisheye.

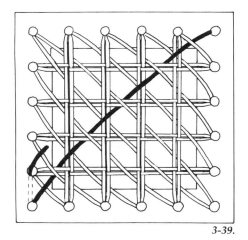

3-39.

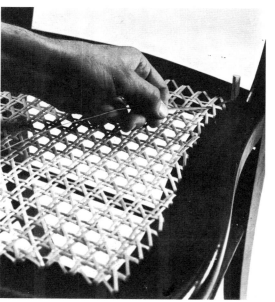

3-40.

48

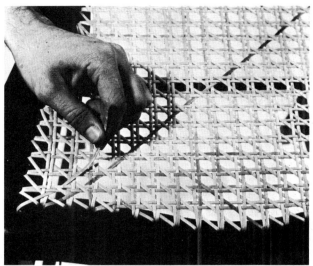

*3-41. The returning strand will form a "fisheye" in the starting corner hole.*
*3-42. As the cane pattern tightens along the rail, use an ice pick to maneuver the strand.*
*3-43. Step Six is complete. There is a "fisheye" in each corner.*

When the cane strand is back at the corner hole and the fisheye is complete, bring the strand up through the adjacent hole on the back rail. Weave another diagonal across in the same manner as before, going under the first diagonal from Step Five, which it meets, then going over the verticals and under the horizontals until the back half is complete. At this stage the tension in the seat becomes substantially greater, so use the ice pick to aid in the tight spots (Figure 3-42).

Weave the front half of the chair, starting at the hole next to the right-hand corner hole. Continue the diagonals to finish Step Six (Figure 3-43). Remember to watch for the skipped and doubled-up holes on the side and front rails.

If the diagonals are properly woven, a series of x's will form as Steps Five and Six cross each other on the rail. The x's are particularly noticeable on the back rail, although they occur on all rails.

Tie off the loose cane strands on the underside of the chair frame. When all the knots are tied and secure, clip the ends of the cane back to about 1 inch (2cm) in length.

**Step Seven**

Binder cane, which is traditionally 1 or 2 sizes larger than the cane used for the seat weaving, is placed around the edge of the chair frame to cover the holes and act as a finished border for the weave. Use one long piece to go around the whole seat frame. If the binder cane is not long enough, or if it breaks while you are using it, it can be spliced. See the end of Step Seven for instructions on how to add on a new piece.

To use binder cane, first soak it in hot water for 15 to 20 minutes to make it pliable. Start the binder in any hole on the right-hand side of the back rail. It should lie parallel to the back rail, with the glossy side up. Bring a piece of regular weaving cane of

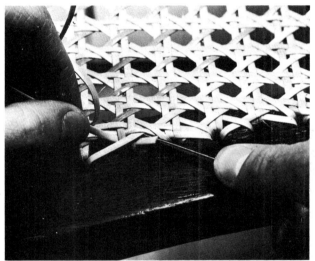

3-41.

3-42.

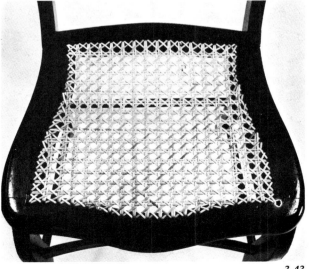

3-43.

3-44.

3-45.

3-46.

*3-44. Insert the binder cane in the back rail. Pull the weaving cane up through a nearby hole and over the binder cane from outside to inside, forming a loop.*

*3-45. To secure the binder cane and ease it into the hole, the hand on top pulls the binder up and the hand below pulls the weaving cane down. Apply pressure alternately, pulling up, then down, and gently rocking the binder into the hole to form a dimple.*

*3-46. After the first loop has been pulled tight, make a second loop in the next hole. Pull each loop tight to secure the binder and form a small dimple.*

good length up through a hole in the center of the back rail, over the top of the binder cane from the outside of the hole, and then back through the same hole, thus forming a loop to secure the binder (Figure 3-44). Pull the loop tight with one hand underneath the chair and the other holding the binder cane in place (Figure 3-45). While the hand underneath pulls the loop tight, the hand on top should gently ease the binder into the hole by slightly lifting it along its length. A small dimple will form in the binding cane.

Continue threading the weaving cane through sequential loops and over the binder around the seat frame. Keep the loops tight, forming little dimples at each hole (Figure 3-46). The corner holes are no different from

3-47.

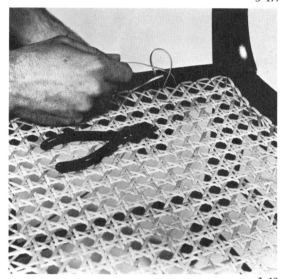

3-48.

**3-47.** *Pull the cane gently around the corner as a dimple is formed in the corner hole.*

**3-48.** *To finish the binder, form a loop in the second-to-last hole to hold both ends of the binder cane in place. This same method can be used to splice a broken binder.*

**3-49.** *Form a loop in the last hole to secure the binder. When the last loop is pulled tight, cut the binder off as close to the last securing loop as possible.*

other holes except that you must pull the binder in a new direction to form the dimple (Figure 3-47). This is easy to do if the cane is wet and pliable.

Cut the beginning of the binder about 2 holes away from the first securing loop. Lay the other end of the binder, which has now traveled around the whole edge of the chair, on top of this loose end. Bind the last 2 holes as before to hold both ends of binder in place (Figure 3-48). The dimple will be a little harder to form because of the double layer. Tie off the ends of the weaving cane on the underside of the chair (Figure 3-50). Cut the end of the binder cane with clippers as close as possible to the final securing loop (Figure 3-49).

3-49.

3-50.

This same method of ending can be used for adding or splicing a new length of binder should the need arise; simply lay the new end on top of the old one and secure the double layer with a loop. It is best to lap the splice over 2 holes.

**3-50.** *Tie off all the loose ends and clip or cut them off next to their securing loops. The cane on the underside of the chair should be secure, and as neat as possible.*
**3-51.** *The finished chair.*

3-51.

# Special Techniques
# in Hand Caning

There are a number of special caning techniques and patterns. In general they tend to be more complicated than the Seven Step method, and you should have a working knowledge of that method before attempting the variant and new patterns illustrated here.

## CURVED RAILS

Chairs with curved or contoured rails (rails not in a flat plane) must be woven with a variation in the order of the seven steps (Figure 4-1). The order of the steps is changed so that the contour of the rail can be maintained and there is not so much slack in the weave that the caner becomes confused as to which strand is which.

### EXAMPLE ONE

The curved rails on this chair demand a variation on the normal Seven Step method: they are still the same seven steps, but their order changes.

**Step One**

Weave from side to side so that the curve of the chair is defined.

**Step Two**

String cane from front to back and *underneath* the side-to-side cane (Figure 4-2).

4-1.

*4-1. The curved rails on this chair demand a variation on the normal Seven Step method. Weave Step One from side to side so that the curve of the chair seat is defined.*
*4-2. Step Two. String cane from front to back and* underneath *the side to side cane.*

4-2.

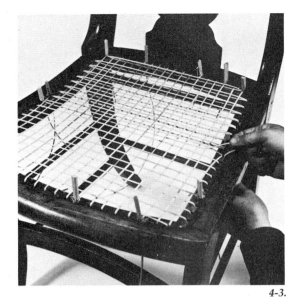

4-3.

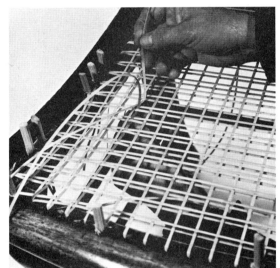

4-4.

4-5.

*4-3. String Step Three from side to side,* underneath *all other cane and in front of the first cane.*
*4-4. Weave Step Four from front to back, just to the right of the second cane. Weave under Step Three and over Step One.*
*4-5. In Steps Five and Six, weave both strands simultaneously to better define the curve of the rail.*

### Step Three

String cane from side to side underneath the previous 2 steps (Figure 4-3). The third step will lie underneath yet be visible (side by side with Step One).

### Step Four

Weave from front to back. The cane of Step Four will lie just to the right of Step Two and go under the cane of Step Three and over the cane of Step One (Figure 4-4).

### Steps Five and Six

Weave both strands simultaneously to help better define the curve of the rail. This is done by first weaving one crossing, or diagonal, with Step Five then weaving another crossing with Step Six (Figure 4-5).

### Step Seven

The binder cane is woven as described. See Step Seven in Chapter Three.

EXAMPLE TWO

Some chairs, especially early American rockers, have a double curved back. This is where the vertical posts form a shallow "S" shape and the horizontal boards in the frame have a slight bow, as in this Lincoln rocker (Figure 4-6).

To start the weaving, first run a number of temporary vertical strands from top to bottom. These strands help define the bow in the horizontal rails of the chair-back frame.

*4-6. For a chair with a double curved back, run a number of temporary vertical strands from top to bottom. These help define the bow in the horizontal rails.*

*4-7. String Step One from side to side behind the temporary verticals. This defines the curve in the vertical rails.*

*4-8. Step Two. String cane vertically and behind the horizontals. Remove the temporary strands; the verticals have now taken over their function.*

*4-9. Weave Step Three from side to side and behind all other cane.*

### Step One

String cane from side to side *behind* the temporary verticals. This step defines the curve in the vertical post in the frame of the chair back (Figure 4-7).

### Step Two

String cane vertically behind the horizontal strands of Step One (Figure 4-8). Remove the temporary vertical strands because the newly strung verticals of Step Two have taken over their function.

### Step Three

String cane from side to side and behind all the other steps (Figure 4-9).

4-6.

4-7.

4-8.

4-9.

55

4-10.

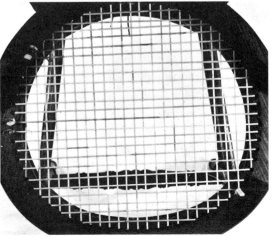

4-11.

*4-10. The completed double curved back.*
*4-11. To begin the round-back chair, weave as usual.*

### Steps Four, Five, Six, and Seven

These steps are woven in the usual manner of the Seven Step method, with the exception that Step Four is woven from top to bottom instead of from side to side (Figure 4-10).

### EXAMPLE THREE

Round chairs are woven following the Seven Step method that other caned chairs use, except that some caners prefer to change the order of the steps. The advantage of caning in the following order is that the early addition of the diagonal strand keeps the strands from the previous 2 steps locked in place. This can be a critical point when weaving a deeply curved back such as is found on a barrel-back or tub chair, where there has to be a lot of slack in the horizontal strands to make the curved surface. Some caners prefer this method for *all* their caning, so it is presented here as an alternative method for you to try.

### Step One

Weave back to front as done in the Seven Step method.

### Step Two

Weave side to side, as previously described (Figure 4-11).

### Step Three

This *was* Step Five. Weave a diagonal from the left-hand rear corner to the right-hand front portion of the seat frame. Be careful

*4-12.* *Weave Step Three (diagonal) under the verticals and over the horizontals.*

*4-13.* *Lay Step Four on top of all other Steps and to the right of Step One.*

*4-14.* *In Step Five, weave under Step One and Three, over Step Four, and in front of Step Two.*

*4-15.* *Make sure you weave* under *the strands of Step Three on the right hand side of the seat. Use an ice pick if need be.*

4-12.

of your hole selection. Weave under the verticals and over the horizontals (Figure 4-12).

## Step Four

This was previously Step Three. Lay cane down from front to back over all other cane (Figure 4-13).

## Step Five

This was previously Step Four. Work from side to side. Weave the strand under the verticals and diagonals, and over the horizontals. Lay the strands in front of and parallel to the previous horizontals (Figures 4-14 and 4-15).

4-13.

4-14.

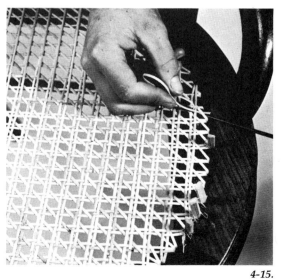

4-15.

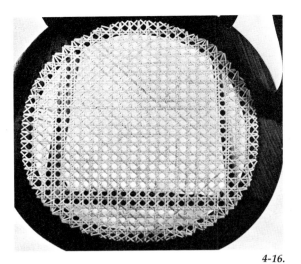

4-16.

*4-16. Weave Step Six over Steps One and Four and under Steps Two and Five.*
*4-17. The finished Spider Weave pattern.*
*4-18. Damaged cane and binding have been removed so that the repair work can be started.*

### Step Six

This is the second diagonal. Weave it under the horizontals and over the verticals (Figure 4-16). Make sure that the 2 diagonal strands slide smoothly through the intersections of the horizontal and vertical pairs. The diagonals should not bind at those intersections.

### Step Seven

Attach the binder cane as in the Seven Step method.

## WEAVING ON CHAIR BACKS

The following weaving patterns are not suitable for seats, since their proportion of cane to space is such that they cannot support very much weight. They are, however, quite adequate for chair backs, and weaving them provides a rewarding experience for the accomplished caner.

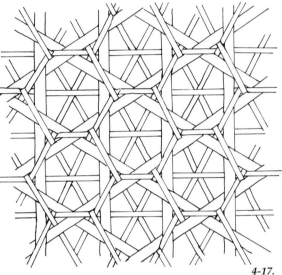

4-17.

### SPIDER WEAVE PATTERN

The Spider Weave (Figure 4-17) involves seven steps and uses 2 sizes of cane plus the binder. There are 3 steps woven with heavier cane and 3 steps woven with a lighter size. Cane sizes generally used are 4mm binder or common cane for the first 3 steps, and fine-fine or superfine for Steps Four, Five, and Six.

Before attempting the Spider Weave, you should have a reasonable knowledge and understanding of the Seven Step method. This is insurance against frustration, as the Spider Weave is difficult.

Setting up the first 3 steps of the Spider Weave is crucial to the success of the overall pattern, as these form a series of hexagonal shapes through which the small cane is woven to create the weblike pattern. The most important part of each step is not to which hole the cane goes but the angle and consistent symmetry of each parallel series.

4-18.

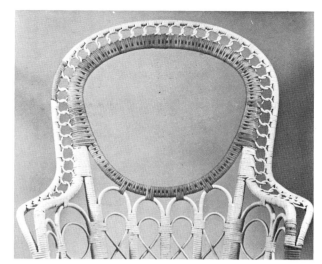

4-19.

*4-19. The wicker frame has been newly wrapped so that there are a number of holes to accommodate the many strands of the Spider Weave pattern.*
*4-20. Step One.*
*4-21. A vertical reference strand and a cardboard tool with 60- and 120-degree angles will help you be consistent.*

*Preparation*

The rocker in Figure 4-18 was originally woven in the Spider Weave pattern and is now about to be repaired in the same pattern. The damaged cane in the middle and the binder around the circumference of the oval have been removed so that the repair work can be started. In Figure 4-19, the new binder cane is finished. (For instructions on this technique, see Chapter 8, under the heading Reed Chain Stitch, and consult Figures 8-53 through 8-55.) The newly wrapped wicker frame has a number of holes to accommodate the many strands of the Spider Weave pattern. Spacing and frequency of the holes on this wrapped wicker frame are an added advantage over the normal wooden frame, where the holes are fixed. On this frame a caner can make holes where they are needed.

*Weaving*

**Step One**

Run a series of 4 or 5 parallel strands, starting at the lower left-hand corner and keeping the strands approximately an inch apart (Figure 4-20). Before finishing Step One, go on to Step Two. This will tell you whether the first step is strung at the correct angle. Weave both steps simultaneously to completion. Construct a 60-degree/120-degree diamond with a vertical reference, as shown in Figure 4-21. This will help you set up for following steps.

**Step Two**

Using heavy cane, lay strands over and across the strands of Step One to form diamond-shaped areas (Figures 4-22 and 4-23). The diamond shapes should have angles of roughly 60 and 120 degrees. These strands should be in a parallel series and approximately 1 inch apart. In order to keep the strands parallel and the angles consistent,

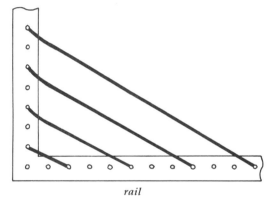

*rail*

4-20.

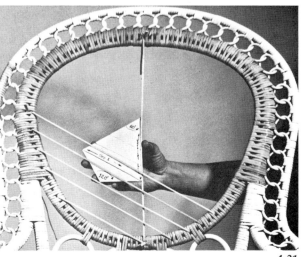

4-21.

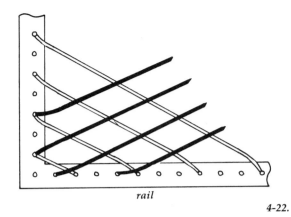

4-23.

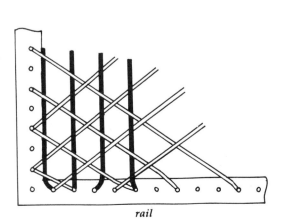

4-24.

**4-22.** *Step Two.*
**4-23.** *In Step Two, run the strands from the top left to the lower right, forming diamonds of 60 and 120 degrees.*
**4-24.** *Step Three.*
**4-25.** *Weave Step Three vertically, going under Step One and over Step Two.*

some strand-by-strand adjustments to the diamonds are usually needed. Holes around the edges will not be used consistently: use the hole that is directly in line with the strands.

### Step Three

This step uses heavy cane and is the first weaving step (Figure 4-24). The diamond shapes become hexagons. Strands are placed vertically within the diamond shapes and run parallel to each other. Weave the cane under the strands of Step One and over those of Step Two (Figure 4-25). In order to keep the cane strands in position, you may have to skip some holes on the rail or veer the cane into the nearest hole.

### Step Four

Use light cane and weave in a horizontal and parallel series. Generally, all the holes in the side rail are used, 1 strand to each hole. Occasionally one may be skipped or strands may double up in others. The weaving pattern is over the intersection of strands of Steps One and Two and under those of Step Three (Figures 4-26 and 4-27).

4-25.

*4-26.* Step Four.
*4-27.* Run Step Four strands horizontally in a parallel series. The strands cross over the intersection of Steps One and Two and under those of Step Three.
*4-28.* Step Five.
*4-29.* In Step Five, run the strands at a steep angle from the bottom left to the upper right.

## Step Five

Use light cane and weave from the bottom left-hand part of the frame towards the upper right-hand portion. The strands will fill most of the holes on the top and bottom rails and about one-half of those on the side rails. They may veer into the hole that keeps the series parallel and the angles consistent.

The weaving pattern is over the intersection of the strands of Steps Two and Three, over those of Step Four, under those of Step One at the triangle, under those of Step Four at the center of the hexagon, and under those of Step One again. Then weave over the strands of Step Four and the intersection of those of Steps Two and Three again (Figures 4-28 and 4-29).

## Step Six

This step uses light cane. The strands lie in a parallel series from the bottom right-hand part of the chair frame to the upper left-hand portion. The top and bottom rails will have most of the holes filled and the sides about half filled.

The weaving pattern is over the intersec-

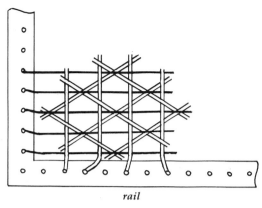

rail

4-26.

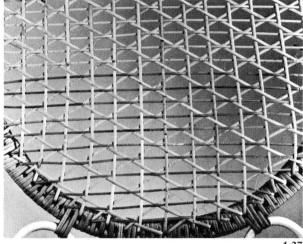

4-27.

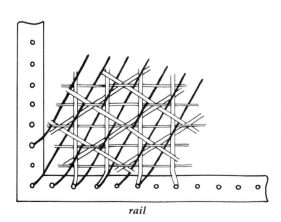

rail

4-28.

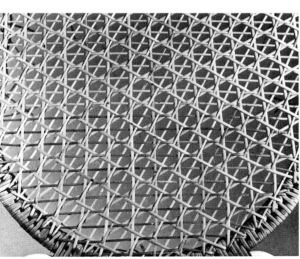

4-29.

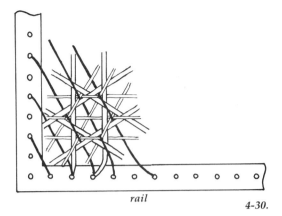

rail

4-30.

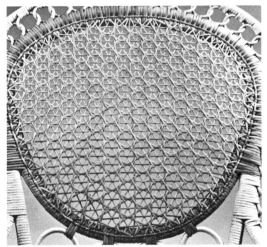

4-31.

4-30. *Step Six.*
4-31. *Weave Step Six at a steep angle from the bottom right to the upper left. Finish with Step Seven, in which the binder is added.*
4-32a. *Cover the exposed loops and knots on the back by braiding a separate strand of cane over the loops and knots in an elongated figure-eight pattern.*
4-32b. *The completed backside of a similar wicker and rattan chair woven in the Spider Web pattern.*

tion of the strands of Steps One and Three, over those of Steps Five and Four, and under Two. Then go under the center of the hexagon and the intersection of the strands of Steps Four and Five, under Step Two, and then over the intersection of Steps Four and Five and One and Three (Figures 4-30 and 4-31).

**Step Seven**

After adding binder cane and tying off the loose ends, a strand of cane is braided around the back to conceal the knots. Insert a new strand of cane under one loop from right to left, crossing over 3 or 4 loops, and inserting it under the fourth loop from the right. Then cross the strand back over itself and insert it just ahead of its last insertion to form a progressively descending figure-eight pattern.

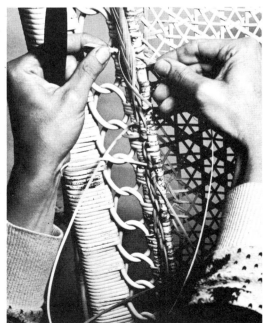

4-32a.

4-32b.

*4-33.* The Star of David, or Snowflake, pattern.
*4-34.* A wicker chair with a heart shaped back is being set up for the Star of David, or Snowflake, pattern. Steps One and Two form a diamond with 60 and 120 degree angles.
*4-35.* Step One.
*4-36.* Step Two.

## STAR OF DAVID, OR SNOWFLAKE, PATTERN

This is a variation of the Spider Weave pattern that creates a 6-pointed star (Figure 4-33). There are 10 steps: 3 in heavy cane (usually 4mm binder or common cane), 6 in lighter cane (usually fine-fine or superfine), and 1 with binder. The 3 steps in heavy cane form the star, and at the center of the star is a hexagon. It is within this hexagon that the 6 steps of light cane meet, forming the radiance of the star.

This is a complicated pattern, so here are a few hints for satisfactory results. Have a working knowledge of the Spider Weave pattern before beginning. The key to the Star of David pattern is to form symmetrical 6-pointed stars with true hexagons at their centers. This done, the other steps will fall into line. To begin, try to visualize the finished pattern starting with Step One. A consistent symmetry will make the pattern "shine."

### Steps One, Two, and Three

Work these in heavy cane, following directions for the 60-degree/120-degree diamond

4-33.

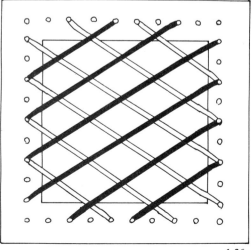

4-34.

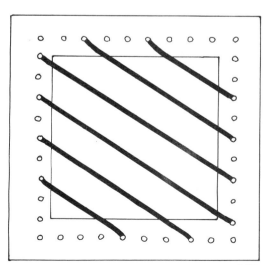

4-35.

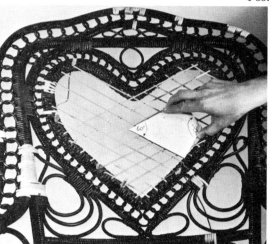

4-36.  63

*4-37. Step Three.*
*4-38. Step Four.*
*4-39. Step Five.*

of the Spider Weave to check your angles (Figures 4-34 through 4-37).

### Step Four

This step uses light cane, and begins the variation. It is similar to Step Four of the Spider Weave, but is woven through every other row of hexagons. Only half as many horizontal strands are woven as were woven in the Spider Weave. Weave under Step Three and over the intersection of Steps One and Two (Figure 4-38).

### Step Five

Continuing with the light cane, work this step like Step Five of the Spider Weave. But once again only half as many strands are woven, as you weave through every other row of hexagons. Make sure you weave through the hexagons defined in Step Four. Weave over the intersection of Steps Two and Three; under Steps One, Four and One again; and then over the intersection of Steps Two and Three (Figure 4-39), and over Four. Then under Step One twice, over Step Four and the intersection of Steps Two and Three, and so on.

### Step Six

With light cane, weave through every other row of hexagons, making sure that you weave through the same hexagons as in Steps Four and Five. Again only half as many strands will be used as in Step Six of the Spider Weave.

Weave over the intersection of Steps One and Three; under Step Two, under Steps Five and Four in the middle of the hexagon, under Step Two, over Steps One and Three, over Four and Five, under Two, and so on (Figure 4-40).

### Step Seven

This step uses light cane, and is woven parallel to Step One between every other pair of Step One strands. Make sure you weave

4-37.

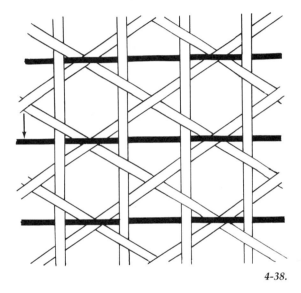

4-38.

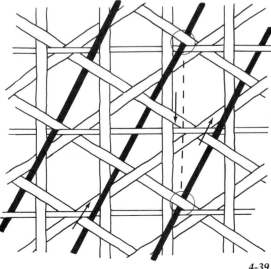

4-39.

*4-40. Step Six.*
*4-41. Steps Seven and Eight.*
*4-42. Step Nine.*

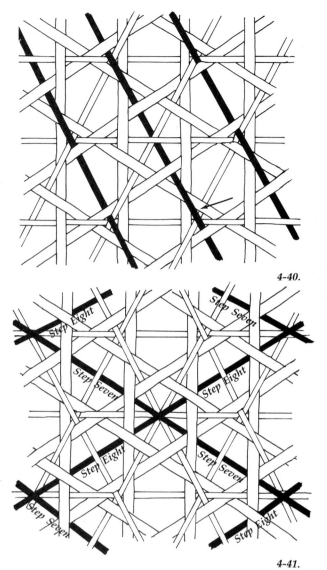

4-40.

4-41.

through the hexagons where the snowflakes or stars are forming. Step Seven should help lock all the strands in place.

Weave under the intersection of Steps Two and Three; under Step Five; under the intersection of Steps Two and Three; over the intersection of Steps Four, Five, and Six; under the intersection of Steps Two and Three; under Step Five; under the intersection of Steps Two and Three; and so on (Figure 4-41).

### Step Eight

Here, light cane is woven parallel to Step Two between every other pair of Step Two strands. It is the mirror image of Step Seven. Make sure you weave through the hexagons, which have the almost-completed stars or snowflakes.

Weave under the intersection of Steps One and Three; under Step Six; under the intersection of Steps One and Three; over the intersection of Steps Four, Five, Six, and Seven; under Steps One and Three; under Step Six; under Steps One and Three; and so on.

### Step Nine

This step, with light cane, locks everything into place. It is woven between every other column delineated by the heavier strands of Step Three and is woven through the radiating hexagons.

Weave vertically under the intersection of Steps One and Two; over the intersection of Steps Four through Eight; under the intersection of Steps One and Two; under Step Four; and under the intersection of Steps One and Two (Figure 4-42).

### Step Ten

Add binder cane, following instructions in the Seven Step method of Chapter 3, and finish the loops on the back, as in Step Eight of the Spider Weave.

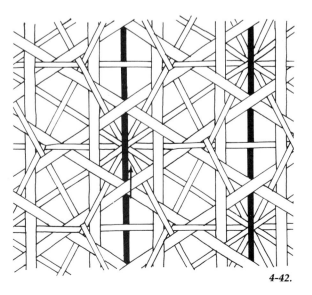

4-42.

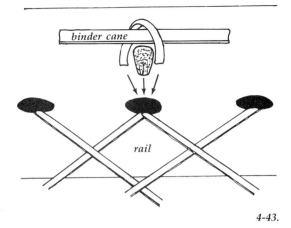

4-43.

4-43. *A small peg holds the precut loop and binder cane.*
4-44. *The cane loops on the backside of this hand-caned Stendig chair are hidden in a groove, which is covered with a wood spline and finished to match the rails.*
4-45. *A blind-caned back without binder. The strands of cane are held in place with glue and pegs.*

## BLIND CANING

Blind caning, or French caning, is the process of caning a panel or chair in which the holes are drilled only partially into the frame rather than all the way through. The cane is secured by pegs in the holes, placed either to one side or underneath the binder cane. Often blind-caned pieces do not have any binder, and the pegs are exposed. Blind caning is used most often on the backs of European chairs, especially those of Spanish and Italian origin.

The advantage of partially drilled holes is that there are no exposed loops on the reverse side of the chair back. In blind caning, though, it is difficult to keep an even tension while weaving, which tends to make a weaker surface. It is for this reason that blind caning is found on chair backs rather than seats, where a stronger attachment is required.

Following are a few points on blind caning:

*Cut each piece of cane to the exact length needed.*
*From start to finish, use pegs to secure the cane ends.*
*Attach the binder cane with small precut loops. Anchor the loops with pegs and glue (Figure 4-43).*

If your chair has partially drilled holes and you do not want to blind cane, drill the holes all the way through; or groove a channel for spline in place of the holes and use prewoven cane.

The Stendig chair from Czechoslovakia, illustrated in Figure 4-44, shows another alternative to having exposed loops on chair backs. It gives the appearance of being blind caned, but it is not. This type of bentwood chair is hand caned normally and has exposed loops on the reverse side of the chair back; the exposed loops are inside a groove, which is then covered with a wood spline.

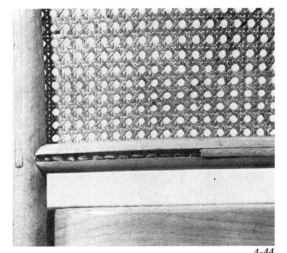

4-44.

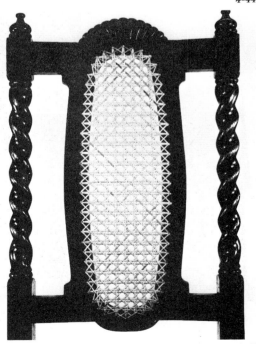

4-45.

66

4-46.

*woven cane*

4-47.

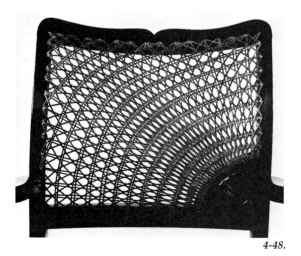

4-48.

**4-46.** *An example of double caning. The cane is woven on the front as well as the back of the chair.*
**4-47.** *Use a handmade semi-spoon-shaped tool to direct the cane to the topside when double caning.*
**4-48.** *The Rising Sun pattern.*

The spline is sanded and finished so that the chair frame appears to be a solid piece of wood. Occasionally you will find a chair back with exposed loops that have been covered with a thin wood veneer. A further variation occurs in Figure 4-45, where no binder is used: pegs alone secure the cane.

DOUBLE CANING

Double caning is the technique of caning both sides of the chair frame (Figure 4-46). If holes are drilled all the way through the chair rails, one side of the chair is hand caned normally and the other side is blind caned. Sometimes both sides of the chair are blind caned in unconnected sets of holes. In either case, the panels are caned separately. In weaving the second side, an awl or a handmade tool is necessary to flick the cane forward after each intersection because it is impossible to get a second hand behind the panel to help in the weaving (Figure 4-47). There are devices specially devised for this purpose.

Double caning is encountered only occasionally, and tends to be found on expensive or fine furniture.

RISING SUN AND SUN RAY PATTERNS

In the Rising Sun pattern (Figure 4-48), Steps One and Three originate at the base and splay to the sides and top, forming a ray pattern. To create the pattern, the lower frame member of your chair must have a highly curved surface in which the holes are

4-49.

4-50.

spaced much closer together than those on the other 3 sides.

Steps One through Four are woven similar to the Seven Step method described in Chapter Three. Steps Two and Four curve concentrically to the base rather than being woven straight across. The diagonal steps are then gentle curves, often doubling up in the holes.

The Sun Ray pattern (Figures 4-49 through 4-51) is an ornate variation on the traditional Seven Step pattern. Generally found on chair backs, it is also present on decorative door panels and headboards. Steps One and Three originate in holes that are drilled very close together—either in a medallion or in the base or corner of the frame—and end in an equal number of holes, drilled very far apart, on the opposite side of the frame. The effect

*4-49. The Sun Ray pattern, with a hand-painted medallion. The diagonals curve all the way to the medallion.*
*4-50. Sun Ray pattern in which the diagonals loop around the inner pair of circles and weave back to the outer frame.*
*4-51. Another Sun Ray variation.*

4-51.

is that Steps One and Three resemble the spokes or rays of a wheel (if a medallion is used), and Steps Two and Four form concentric circles, ovals, or parts of circles around the medallion or curved base or corner.

The Sun Ray pattern is much more difficult to do than the Rising Sun. It's best to carefully photograph or chart the pattern before the old cane is cut away. To hold the medallion in place, suspend it with string from the top and bottom and the 2 sides, or clamp a piece of wood to the back of the chair and clamp the medallion in place. When you have partially completed Steps One and Three and there are sufficient strands to hold the medallion in place, remove the supports. If the holes in the medallion are drilled all the way through, small nails can be used to secure the medallion to a piece of wood (Figure 4-52).

When setting up Steps One and Three be sure to stagger the strands so that all the spaces between the holes on the back of the medallion have a loop of cane. This little zigzag line of cane loops adds to the professional look of the product, important to all accomplished caners. It should also be noted that every hole in the medallion is used in Step One (Figure 4-53). The medallion is often blind caned so that the zigzag line on the back will be absent. If you plan to blind cane, do not drill the holes all the way through, as this is likely to split the medallion.

Weave Steps Two and Four in concentric circles or ovals around the medallion (Figure 4-54). Each strand makes a complete circle and ends by overlapping itself past several intersections. From the original caned back, you should be able to tell how many pairs of circles there must be. Generally, the pairs are between ½ inch and 1 inch apart. The corners will have 2 or 3 pairs of arcs to fill out the back pattern.

The Sun Ray and Rising Sun patterns can

4-52.

4-53.

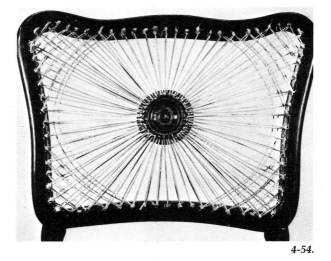

4-54.

4-52. *One way to suspend the medallion is by clamping it to a board that is temporarily clamped to the chair frame.*
4-53. *For Step One, use every hole in the medallion.*
4-54. *Steps One and Three support the medallion while you weave Steps Two and Four alternately around the medallion.*

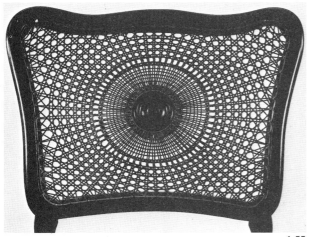

4-55.

*4.55. A completed Sun Ray pattern in which many slight variations in texture can be achieved.*
*4-56. A patch in which individual pieces of cane are spliced in to repair the damaged area.*

length of cane. With a blind binder, the loops are cut to fit each hole and as they secure the binder the pegs secure them.

SPLICE PATCH

One final technique that is used for either the Seven Step pattern or any of the other patterns encountered is a splice patch, in which a small hole or flaw in the seat surface is patched with individually cut pieces of cane. These are then woven into the damaged area. Damaged strands are wet, then replaced one at a time to keep the pattern from unraveling. Leave at least 3 inches of overlap past the damaged area to allow the newly spliced cane enough tension to stay in place (Figure 4-56).

be completed with a regular binder or blind binder, or the cane can simply be secured with small pegs and glue (Figure 4-55). A blind binder is a binder attached to the seat frame by the use of individual precut loops of cane and pegs specially fitted to each hole. (See the section in this chapter entitled Blind Caning.) Normally, the binder is attached to the seat frame by loops of a continuous

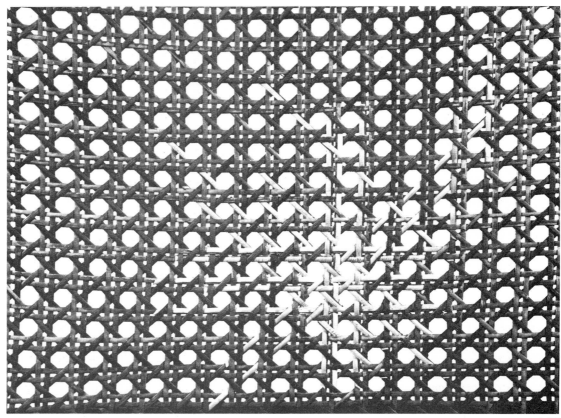

4-56.

# Rushwork

## FIBER RUSH WEAVING

Fiber rush is tough-grade paper fiber that is twisted into a long strand. It is quite strong and durable, and is a good imitation of natural rush (twisted cattail leaves). Fiber rush is easy to obtain and use and has the added benefit of being inexpensive. Even a beginner can do wonderful work with it, provided a few simple directions are followed. It is much easier to use than natural rush and is therefore more desirable when restoring more common furniture. Quality antique furniture however, should be restored with natural rush (discussed later in this chapter) to preserve its value and authenticity.

### Square Seats

TOOLS AND MATERIALS NEEDED

*Hammer*
*File or wood rasp*
*Spray mister*
*Mat knife*
*Hand or spring clamp*
*Screwdriver or block of wood*
*Paint brush*
*Ruler or tape measure*
*Carpet tacks, #3*
*Cardboard*
*Clear shellac*
*Alcohol or shellac thinner*
*Colored varnish (optional)*
*Rush (2 lbs. per chair)*

Some substitutions of these materials can be made to suit your own project. Any cutting blade will do in place of the mat knife. Colored varnish is optional. The spring clamp will act as an extra hand.

Although 2 pounds of fiber rush is suggested for the average chair, there is no method of determining the exact amount a chair will need. Common sense and/or experience will tell you, or your supplier may have reasonable advice.

Fiber rush is usually sold by the pound, often in 2-pound coils. It comes in 3 sizes and colors: $\frac{4}{32}$ inch, for fine work as found on small Windsor or Danish chairs; $\frac{5}{32}$ inch, for most chairs; and $\frac{6}{32}$ inch, for large seats and porch furniture. It is available in Kraft brown, golden yellow, and a multicolored golden yellow with blue and green flecks. The Kraft brown rush, which became available during the paper shortages of the mid 1970s, is the least durable. We use golden yellow for all our fiber-rush work.

### PREPARATION

Rushwork is usually done on square seat frames including those chairs that have a slightly longer front rail. It is most commonly done on chairs with dowel rails although not always, as in the case of a chair where the seat frame is made of flat board rails that

5-1.

5-2.

*5-1. A standard ladder-back chair with 4 round rails made for rush seating. The front and back rails are set somewhat lower in the chair frame.*
*5-2. Roughening the outer edge of the side rails with a rasp or file keeps the rush from slipping on the rail.*

have been indented to accommodate fiber rush.

Once all the tools and materials have been gathered, you are ready to begin. Make sure that the chair is clean of dust and that all tacks and old nails are removed. If the chair is going to be refinished, this is the time to do it. Repairs to cracked or split rails or joints should be made now. Fiber rush exerts a tremendous amount of pressure on a chair frame and will increase the chances of damage to already weak or broken parts. Begin on a strong, sturdy chair (Figure 5-1) with sound parts so you won't have to stop in the middle and pull out all your work to make a repair.

Before you begin weaving, it may be necessary to roughen or notch the outside of the 2 side rails (Figure 5-2). This helps keep the rush from slipping along the side rails toward the back as you weave, and is especially necessary for chairs with curved rails. Be careful not to notch too deeply. The point is to keep the rush from slipping along the rail, not to make grooves for each strand of rush.

## WEAVING

The key to a successful fiber-rush seat is to keep a consistent symmetry and tension at each and every corner. Do this by weaving loosely around the chair then going back and tightening each corner in succession, using the hand clamp as you go.

### Step One

The extra spaces near the front 2 corners are called fill-in corners or, in England, gussets—a term borrowed from sewing to indicate a V-shaped or triangular insert. Because rush weaving is done in a square or right-angle pattern, these corners, caused by the chair's front rail being wider than the back, must be filled in before the main weaving begins. This is called squaring the weave.

To determine the size of the fill-in corners, measure the lengths of the back and front rails. Subtract the length of the back rail from the length of the front rail (Figure 5-3). The difference is the amount of extra space along the front rail. Divide this measurment in half, and you have the size of each fill-in corner. Take this figure and measure inward from each of the 2 front corners. Mark the spot lightly with a pencil along the front rail.

Also measure the length of the side rail. If the side rail is longer than the averaged lengths of both front and back rails, the chair is termed a deep-seated chair. For example, if the back rail is 12 inches, the front rail is 16 inches, and the side rail is longer than 14 (12 plus 16, divided by 2) inches, the chair is a deep-seated chair. A special weaving pattern will be needed to make a comfortable seat. (Instructions for rushing a deep-seated chair are given at the end of this chapter. Read the section before continuing.)

Once you have determined the size of the fill-in corners, begin weaving. Cut off several pieces of fiber rush from the main coil. Each piece should be 2 to 4 times the length of the front rail. Take one length and mist it with the sprayer to make it more pliable. With a tack, attach it to the inside of the left-hand rail about 2 inches away from the front left-hand corner (Figure 5-4). If the chair is made of hardwood, fastening the tack may be difficult and you may have to tie the rush with a piece of tough string or nylon fishing line. This is also suggested to avoid damaging a particularly fragile antique piece.

### Step Two

Take the loose end of the rush and pull it over, around, and underneath the front rail. Then pull it up over itself and around and under the left-hand rail, headed in the direction of the right-hand rail (Figures 5-5 and 5-6).

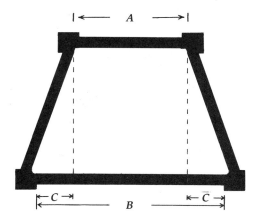

5-3.

5-4.

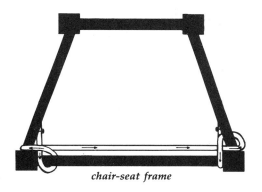

*chair-seat frame*

5-5.

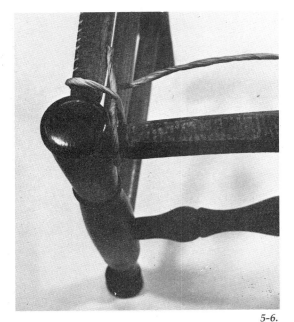

5-6.

*5-6. Weave fill-in strands at the front right corner. The rush goes over itself and around and under the rail.*
*5-7. Attach the second fill-in strand to the inside of the left-hand rail, just behind the first tack.*
*5-8. An example of a typical seat with fill-in corners finished. The rush is neatly compacted at right angles.*
*5-9. The fill-in corners are complete and the rush is evenly compacted against the corners to keep the right angles accurate.*

Pull the end of the fiber rush across to the right-hand rail, then over, around, and underneath the right-hand rail. Continue pulling the rush strand up over itself, then around, and underneath the front rail. Pull the rush taut and into position and tack it to the inside of the right-hand side rail. Cut off any excess rush close to the tack.

Take the second piece of lightly dampened rush and tack it just behind the first tack (Figure 5-7). Then repeat the same weaving pattern as before. Continue adding, weaving, and tacking additional strands until the corners are filled in and the rush reaches the pencil mark on the front rail. At this point the empty space on the front rail should equal the length of the back rail (Figures 5-8 and 5-9).

5-7.

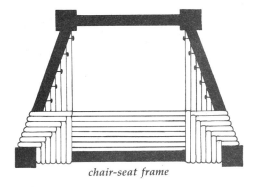

*chair-seat frame*

74

5-8.

5-9.

*5-10. Hold the rush taut with one hand while the thumb and forefinger of the other pinch the rush strand into a right angle at the point where it crosses over itself. To increase control, hold the chair firmly between your legs.*
*5-11. Compact the first few fill-in strands against the front post with a hammer and a screwdriver.*
*5-12. The weaving pattern for a square or rectangular chair. The motion repeats at each corner.*

5-10.

There are several points to consider when doing the fill-in corners: (1) Start and maintain a series of right angles in the weaving pattern at the corners. They create the symmetry in the weave and are crucial to its overall pattern and appearance. Use your thumb and forefinger to press the rush over itself in a right angle while your other hand holds the rush tight (Figure 5-10). (2) As the weaving progresses, compact the fiber rush strands together along the rails to help tighten any looseness in the weave and maintain the right angles in the corners. Compact the strands by placing a screwdriver or block of wood perpendicular to the rail next to the rush. Then tap it smartly with a hammer (Figure 5-11). Do not, by forcing the strands on top of each other, compact the rush so much that it creates lumps. If you use a screwdriver, be sure that the flat point is next to the wooden rail so as not to tear the rush in the process of moving it. Compact the weave every 2 or 3 courses so that no slack develops in the strands.

### Step Three

Cut off approximately 25 feet of fiber rush and coil it for easier handling. Using this length helps avoid twisting and lumping and facilitates adding on more lengths. Mist this coil of rush with water to make it more pliable. Tack one end to the inside of the left-hand rail near the back corner. Weave it around the front left corner, as with the fill-in pieces. Next, move on to the right-hand corner. Instead of tacking the rush to the right-hand rail, weave it around the back corner in exactly the same pattern as the front corners (Figures 5-12 and 5-13).

Weave the rush over, around, and under the back rail near the right corner. Now bring the rush up over itself and around the right-hand rail near the back corner. It is now headed in the direction of the back left-hand corner.

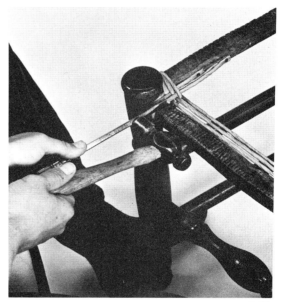

5-11.

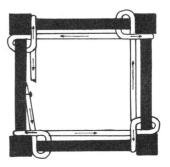

5-12.

75

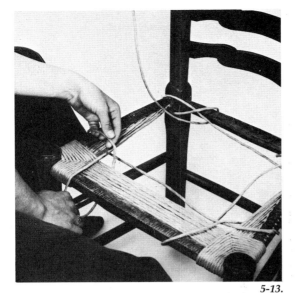

5-13.

*5-13. For the first full course, weave the rush loosely around all the corners. Then tighten each corner individually.*
*5-14. Use a square knot to add another length of rush. Tie the knot so that it will lie midway between the corners of the seat, where it will be hidden by later courses.*
*5-15. Pull the square knot tight and clip off the loose ends.*

Complete the last corner by bringing the rush over the top and then around and under the left-hand rail. Finally, bring the rush strand up over itself and then around and underneath the back rail near the back left-hand corner. One complete weave is finished, and the rush should now be headed in the direction of the front rail. It is usually easier to weave once around all the corners loosely using the spring clamp to keep the strand taut, and then go back to the spring clamp, release it, and tighten the loose rush at each corner with your fingers to make it square.

Continue this pattern until about two-thirds of the rail surface is covered. Remember 3 points as you weave:

*Every 2 or 3 times around, compact the strands along the rail to maintain right angles and avoid looseness.*
*Keep the right angles accurate.*
*If you run out of rush, simply tie another piece on with a square knot (Figure 5-14). Attach the new piece midway between the corners so that the knot will be covered by later weaving (Figures 5-15 and 5-16).*

5-14.

5-15.

*5-16.* A spring (or hand) clamp is like another hand: it holds the rush firmly while you tie off the square knot and clip the excess cane.

*5-17.* Stuff the underside of the chair with 3 or 4 layers of cardboard. Clip the tips of the cardboard triangles to add to the layering effect as well as to leave space at the center of the chair for later weaving.

*5-18.* The topside of the chair is also stuffed with several layers of cardboard, clipped in the same fashion.

## Step Four

Begin stuffing the seat when approximately two-thirds of the rail surface is covered. Kraft paper or newspaper can be used, but corrugated cardboard seems to work best to make the seat both comfortable and pleasing in appearance.

Place the stuffing in layers, first on the underside and then on the topside of the chair seat. Cut the cardboard in the shape of a triangle so that it will fit neatly between the layers of the weave (Figures 5-17 and 5-18). The corrugations of the cardboard should run parallel to the rail it is placed against. Place several layers of cardboard along each rail. Make sure each piece fits snug. Each succeeding piece of cardboard should be somewhat smaller than the preceding one. The layers in the stuffing create a flat, comfortable seat. Clip off the tips of the triangles near the center of the chair to help the layered effect as well as to allow space for future weaving. The front and back rails may require more layers than the side rails because they are often set lower in the chair frame. You will know you have enough stuffing

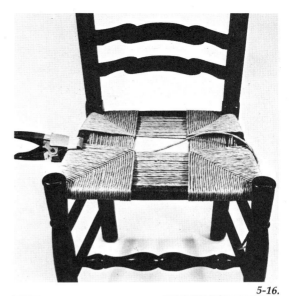

5-16.

5-17.

77

5-18.

5-19.

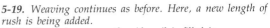
**5-19.** *Weaving continues as before. Here, a new length of rush is being added.*

**5-20.** *The last space on the side rail is filled in.*

**5-21.** *An example of the figure-eight pattern on the bridge. The rush goes around the rail, then up through the center and around the opposite rail and so on until the space is filled.*

**5-22.** *An example of the figure-eight pattern to be used after the last space on the side rails has been filled. In this example the rush strand goes first to the back rail. On your chair, you may weave toward the front rail. The pattern is the same: over the rail, underneath, up through the middle, and around the opposite rail.*

**5-23.** *Tack the fiber-rush strand to the underside of the rail when the weaving is finished.*

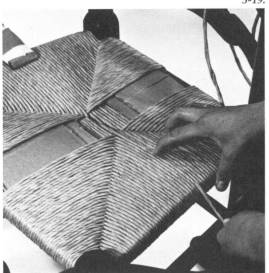

5-20.

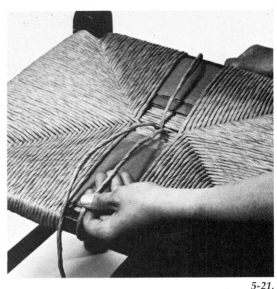

5-21.

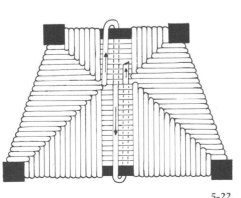

5-22.

5-23.

*5-24. Cut the rush off approximately 2 inches after the tack, and tuck the loose end under a neighboring strand.*
*5-25. Rub the screwdriver handle over the completed seat to even out any bumps or spaces in the weaving.*

when the unevenness is gone and any looseness in the strands has been taken up. The stuffing is finished when all the strands are lying next to each other on the same smooth, level surface.

## Step Five

Once the stuffing is in place, continue the weaving as before, adding extra lengths of rush as they are needed (Figure 5-19); do this by tacking the old end and the new end to the underside of, preferably, the back rail. Try to finish with one long length of rush because it is difficult to hide knots as the weaving closes up. When the side rails have been filled (Figure 5-20), a new type of weaving pattern, a figure-eight weave, is begun. This is called the bridge.

## Step Six

To fill in the front and back rails, a figure-eight pattern is used. The figure eight starts at either the front or back rail, depending on which direction the rush is heading. The process is called bridging, and the area to be woven is called the bridge.

Bring the rush strand up, over, around, and underneath the rail. Pull the rush up through the center hole in the direction of the opposite rail, either front or back depending on which direction you started in (Figures 5-21 and 5-22). Then repeat the same motion, to complete the figure eight. Continue this pattern until both the front and back rails are filled. They will fill up simultaneously if you have done the fill-in corners correctly. When the last bit of space on the rails is filled, turn the chair over and tack the rush to the underside of the nearest rail (Figure 5-23). Cut the end of the rush about 3 inches past the point where the tack was set. Unravel the fiber rush end and use a screwdriver to tuck it up under a neighboring strand (Figure 5-24).

5-24.

5-25.

## Step Seven

Set the chair right side up and in front of you. With the handle of the screwdriver, rub over any lumps or spaces in the fiber-rush strands (Figure 5-25). This burnishing action serves two purposes: (1) it corrects the unevenness in the twisted strands, leveling highs and lows caused by inconsistent tension when the strands were pulled taut, and (2) it molds the strands together to fill in the gaps between them. Smooth the rush covering the rail by tapping lightly with a hammer.

79

5-26.

5-27.

5-26. *Brush on shellac to seal the rush and preserve the seat.*
5-27. *A deep-seated chair woven with a vertical bridge. Because the bridge is vertical, it will not shape itself to the posterior with the same facility as the chair in Figure 5-28.*
5-28. *A deep-seated chair with an extra figure eight in the weaving pattern.*

## Finishing

The last step is to seal the entire fiber-rush surface. First brush away any dust or other debris that may have accumulated on the chair during the weaving. Next, prepare a solution of 3 parts alcohol and 1 part shellac. The alcohol will evaporate and dry the shellac fairly rapidly. Brush one light coat on both the top and bottom of the seat (Figure 5-26). When it dries, brush on another light coat. The shellac coat prevents damage from spills and dirt and prolongs the life of the seat. Varnish can also be used as a sealer.

The fiber rush will turn a mellow tan with time. If you don't wish to wait, there are many colored varnishes available to enhance the shade of the rush. *The seat should be sealed before it is colored.*

## Deep-seated Chairs

A deep-seated chair is one in which the side rail is longer than the averaged lengths of the front and back rails (Figures 5-3 and 5-27). If it is woven with the normal pattern, the front and back rails will fill up before the side rails. This causes 2 problems: (1) the horizontal pattern of the bridge becomes vertical (front to back), and (2) the bridge is formed in the middle of the seat instead of slightly to the back, as it should be. On the face of it these problems would not seem to matter much. However, the chair is considerably more comfortable when these 2 sit-

uations are avoided, and the best way to avoid them is to plan so that the side rails fill up first.

The weaving pattern for a deep-seated chair is the same as normal except that a figure eight is woven between the front 2 corners (Figure 5-28). That is, for every wrap around the front rails, the side rails are wrapped twice.

Start at the front left-hand corner using the normal pattern. Move across to the right-hand corner and wrap the rush around the right-hand rail. Then come *directly back* to the

5-28.

*deep-seated chair frame*

5-29.

*5-29.* The weaving pattern for a deep-seated chair. The rush circles the side rails twice, thereby filling them at a faster rate than normal.
*5-30.* A deep-seated chair with 2 figure eights added to the normal weaving pattern.
*5-31.* The weaving pattern for a triangular seat. It is similar to the normal pattern but has 1 less corner post.
*5-32.* Two completed triangular stools.

left-hand rail and over and around it. Now the rush is headed back in the direction of the right-hand rail again (Figure 5-29). Resume the normal pattern. By adding a figure eight each time you are at the front 2 corners, the side rail will fill up at a faster rate. This moves the bridge toward the back of the seat (Figure 5-30). Determining when to stop adding extra figure eights in the pattern is a matter of judgment. The figure eight should drop out of the pattern any time after the side rails have less space on them than the front and back rails.

## Triangular Seats

Triangular seats (Figures 5-31 and 5-32) are no more difficult than 4-sided rush seats.

5-30.

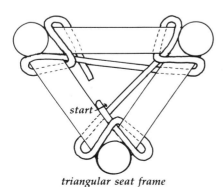

*start*

*triangular seat frame*

5-31.

81

5-32.

5-33.

*5-33. A completed Windsor chair with a rush seat.*
*5-34. To allow for the weaving, release the back from the seat by removing 4 screws hidden under wooden plugs.*
*5-35. A mule-eared chair finished with a rush seat.*

The weaving pattern makes use of the same configuration, and the corners are formed in the same manner. You still weave to the adjacent rail, moving clockwise on the seat frame. On a triangular seat frame you do not form right angles; instead, if the 3 sides of the chair are of equal length, the angles approximate 120 degrees.

## Windsor Chairs

Windsor chairs (a style of wooden chair popular in the eighteenth century, with spreading legs, a spindle back and often as not a rush seat) present a new problem to the weaver (Figure 5-33). On a Windsor chair, the back must be removed in order to start the weaving. Occasionally wood covering the side rails will also have to be removed. Screws that hold the back and the side in place are often hidden under wooden plugs, so don't let the fact that screws are not visible confound you (Figure 5-34).

Another problem associated with some Windsor chairs is a curved rail. The fiber rush tends to slip down to the center of the curve, so rasp the rail to increase friction on

5-35.

screw

dowel

5-34.

5-36.

*5-36. A wicker corner chair with a 4/32-inch rush seat.*
*5-37. The dried cattail leaves are sprinkled with water, covered with plastic, and allowed to soak up moisture over night.*

the rush. (See Figure 5-2, shown earlier in the chapter.) Once the seat frame is accessible, the weaving follows the normal fiber rush procedure (Figures 5-35 and 5-36).

## NATURAL RUSH WEAVING

Natural or genuine rush is twisted from the leaves of cattails. It is harvested in the late summer and early fall, when the leaves are the longest and before the autumn rains. The leaves should be green, with the occasional tip turning brown.

Before use, the leaves are separated and dried in a dark room or garage for several weeks. Natural rush is soaked in hot tap water for 4 to 5 hours before it is ready to be used. It can also be sprinkled with water and left to soak overnight (Figure 5-37). The thicker, butt ends are cut off and used later on for stuffing. Some weavers also flatten the leaf by running it between thumb and forefinger to remove the air pockets within (Figure 5-39).

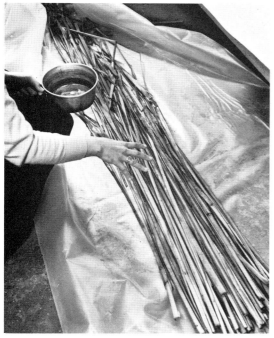

5-37.

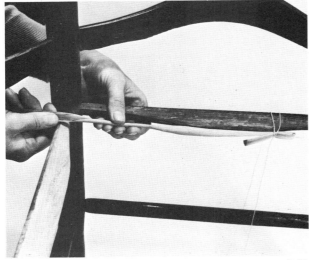

5-38.

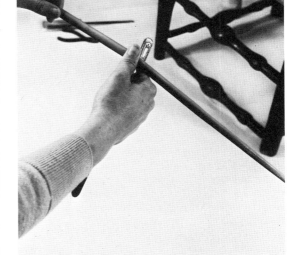

5-39.

5-42.

5-43.

**5-38.** The first strand, consisting of 2 leaves placed butt end to tip end, is tied to the side rail. Using the thumb and middle finger, carefully roll the strand back and forth to form an evenly twisted roll.

**5-39.** Each leaf must have air forced out of the cells by pulling it between the thumb and the dull side of a table knife. As air is expelled, "pops" will be heard.

**5-42.** The rush has wrapped around the 4 corners 5 or 6 times. Notice that the rush need only be twisted carefully at the corners. The "open" part of the seat will be covered with successive courses of rush.

**5-43.** A natural-rush seat half completed. Here a new leaf is added by inserting the butt end of the leaf into the corner as the strand heads for the front rail (lower right corner of photo).

*5-40.* A new leaf is added as the strand comes out of the corner heading toward the opposite rail. Here the butt end is inserted into the corner where the leaf will wrap around the existing strand a few times to anchor itself. The butt end will hang down a few inches below the seat, to be trimmed off later. To maintain a consistent strand, drop a short leaf from the rolled strand when adding a new leaf.

*5-41.* Here the new leaf has been wrapped around the strand. The strand can be brought across the open seat untwisted until it reaches the opposite corner where the twisting must begin again.

Weaving one leaf at a time makes a thin strand, and is the recommended technique for beginners (Figure 5-38). The leaves are started at their tip ends and woven by twisting the strand in the form of a straight candy cane. A new strand is added by overlapping the old end with the new tip. It is done when the strand is at the bottom of the seat, so that the join will not show on the topside (Figure 5-40). Some weavers recommend a square knot for adding new lengths to the strand already in progress.

The pattern for weaving natural rush is the pattern from which fiber-rush seats originate. They are the same, with the exception that natural rush tends to make a bulkier seat with slightly larger and less consistent strands.

Weaving natural rush requires consummate skill and patience, and we recommend that the weaver have a good knowledge of fiber rush and the requirements of the task at hand before attempting to weave a seat.

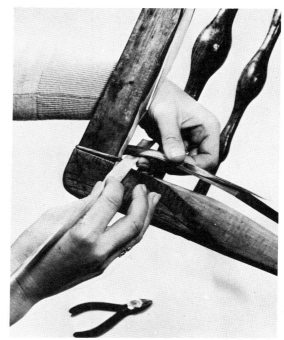

*5-40.*

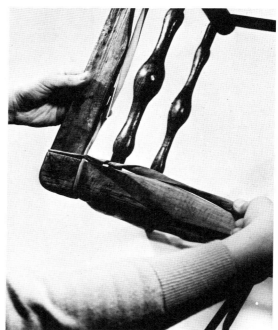

*5-41.*

# Working With Splint,
# Shaker Tape, and Rawhide

This chapter details instructions on 3 types of chair seating. They are grouped together not so much because the techniques are the same but because they are all applied to the same kind of piece: the dowel-railed chair.

Dowel-railed chairs are ubiquitous, and come in all sizes and shapes. The standard feature, however—whether the chairs are mule eared or of the ordinary kitchen variety—is the 4 round rails of the seat frame.

## SPLINT WEAVING

Splints were originally hand split from white oak, hickory, or ash. The homemade-chair maker would often split his own splints with which to weave (or, in the Appalachian term, "bottom") his chair seat. Splints were easy to weave and of the same material as the chair. They were found locally and were therefore affordable for the country craftsman (Figures 6-1 and 6-2).

Today handsplit splints are rarely found, and the most commonly used material for a splint seat is flat reed or wide binder cane, although hickory, oak, or ash splints can also be used.

Weaving with splint is simple to do and very quick to complete. Any chair with 4 dowels for seat-frame rails can be splint woven. It is often found on "country chairs" or obviously handmade chairs. The weaving pattern itself is a simple plaiting similar to that done by children weaving construction-paper place mats. A splint seat is exceptionally strong and durable and will remain a comfortable seat for many years if it is properly cared for.

### TOOLS AND MATERIALS NEEDED

*Right-angle square*
*Stapler*
*Mat knife*
*Shears or heavy scissors*
*Hand clamp*
*Hammer*
*Carpet tacks, #3*
*Sandpaper, fine (220 grit)*
*Splints or binder cane*

All the tools needed for splint weaving are found in most homes. The materials are obtainable through many suppliers. Oak, hickory, and ash splints are generally stocked although their supply is occasionally irregular. Hickory and oak splints are hand cut even to this day, and their widths are not consistent; check what is available and adjust according to the chart below. Machine-cut ash splints are available in ⅝- and 1-inch widths only. This is also true for Shaker tapes. The amount of material needed for your chair—be it hickory, oak, machine-cut ash or Shaker tapes—can be determined by the chart.

6-1.

6-1. *New cane chair seat being made near Pembroke Farms, North Carolina. M. Post Wolcott (1938). (Library of Congress collection)*

6-2. *Hickory being split for chair bottom in Arkansas Hills (Ozarks) near Seligman, Missouri. Dorothea Lange (1938). (Library of Congress collection)*

6-2.

Flat reed, which is most commonly used for splint weaving, is the inner core of the rattan palm cut either flat or slightly oval. An easy method of determining the top or face side of the flat reed is to bend it into a loop (Figure 6-3). If small splinters are raised at the point of the bend, then you are looking at the underside of the splint. It is available in widths of ¼ inch, ⅜ inch, ½ inch, ⅝ inch, and 1 inch.

Binder cane is cut from the peel or bark of the rattan palm and is available in widths of 4mm, 5 to 5½mm, 6mm, and 8 to 10mm. It is only available in millimeter widths, and the measurements just given are termed narrow, medium, and extra wide.

The following chart will help you determine the amount of material needed to cover your chair:

| Size of Seat (in inches) | Amount of ½-inch splint | Amount of ⅝-inch splint | Amount of 1-inch splint |
|---|---|---|---|
| 13 × 10 | 84 feet | 72 feet | 42 feet |
| 15 × 12 | 120 feet | 102 feet | 60 feet |
| 18 × 14 | 156 feet | 132 feet | 78 feet |
| 19 × 16 | 198 feet | 168 feet | 99 feet |
| 21 × 17 | 228 feet | 192 feet | 114 feet |
| 22 × 19 | 252 feet | 213 feet | 126 feet |

PREPARATION

Soak the splint, flat reed, or binder cane in hot (140 degrees F/60 degrees C), tap water half an hour. Woody splints, hickory, ash, and oak need to soak much longer. Oak and ash should soak between an hour and 2 hours, hickory needs to soak for 4 hours or more. If your material has soaked long enough, it will be pliable and easy to work with.

**6-3.** *When a flat reed splint is bent at a sharp angle, tiny, splinterlike hairs will be raised on the* bottom.

WEAVING

**Step One**

Because the front rail of most chairs is longer than the back rail, several fill-in lengths will be needed to cover the extra space at the front corners. This is true of the chair illustrated here. To determine the size of the fill-in corners, measure the length of the back rail and the length of the front rail. Subtract one from the other, which gives you the amount of extra space along the front rail. Divide this figure in half to determine the size of each fill-in corner. Measure the distance inward from each of the 2 front corners and mark it lightly with a pencil along the front rail (Figures 6-4 and 6-5).

Or, you can measure the extra length on the front rail with a right-angle square. Line the top of the square parallel with the back rail and adjacent to the back corner. With a pencil, mark the point at which the square crosses the front rail. This method can be done at both corners.

6-4.

6-5.

6-6.

6-7.

*6-4. Marking the fill-in corners with a ruler.*
*6-5. With a right-angle square and a pencil, mark the length of the back rail on the front rail.*
*6-6. To begin the warping of the chair, tack the end of the splint to the inside left-hand rail near the back corner.*
*6-7. Pull the splint around the front rail adjacent to the pencil mark.*

**Step Two**

Tack or tie the end of the splint to the inside of the left-hand rail near the back corner. Make sure the correct side of the splint is facing out. An easy way of recognizing top or face side of the flat reed is to bend it into a loop. If small splinters are raised at the point of the bend, you are looking at the underside of the splint (Figure 6-6).

Pull the splint over the top and around the front rail next to the pencil mark. Then pull the splint underneath the back rail and then around it next to the back corner (Figure 6-7). Continue wrapping splint around the front and back rails in this fashion until the entire back rail is covered and the space between the pencil marks on the front rail is filled.

6-8.

6-9.

*6-8. Add new lengths of splint by overlapping the ends 6 to 8 inches and then stapling them together. The staple prongs should be toward the inside of the seat.*

*6-9. When the back rail is covered, stop the warping and tack the end to the right-hand rail near the back corner.*

*6-10. Start the first weaver, a fill-in strand, at the back of the chair. Go under the first warp strand, then over 3, under 3, and so on to the opposite side. At the right-hand side, tuck the weaver under to the inside of the seat.*

In most cases you will need to add new lengths of flat reed or binder cane as you weave. Simply staple a new reed to the end of the old length, with an overlap of 6 to 8 inches (Figure 6-8). Add new lengths on the bottom of the seat and make sure the staple prongs face the inside of the seat so that you don't cut your fingers later on. Most weavers call these splints that are woven between the front and the back rails the warp. The splints that are woven from side to side are called the weft, or the weavers. When the warping is finished, hold the end of the splint in position with a hand clamp (Figure 6-9).

**Step Three**

The weavers, or splints woven through the warp, are perpendicular to the warp. Their movement is essentially over 3 warp strands and under 3, over 3 and so on, the first being a fill in. The herringbone pattern is created by shifting the position of the units of 3 on each successive crossing. Start at the back left-hand corner, insert the splint face up *under 1 warp* strand, then start weaving the over 3, under 3 pattern until it reaches the right-hand rail. The weaver may end at the right-hand rail in an incomplete unit of 3. This is common (Figure 6-10). Don't attach this first splint to the rail, as its ends are woven (tucked) into the chair seat. The tension of the warp will hold it in place.

Next, take a new piece of splint and weave, making a second crossing on the top-side of the chair (Figure 6-11). The weaving

90

6-10.

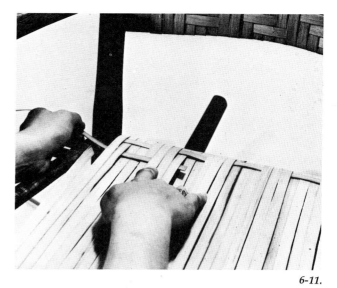

6-11.

*6-11. The second weaver, a new splint, moves under 2 warp strands, then over 3, under 3, and so on. Pull the weaver around the right-hand rail and continue weaving on the bottom portion of the seat.*

*6-12. The second weaver in place on the top of the seat.*

*6-13. Weave the splint on the underside of the seat over 3, under 3, and so on, similar to that on the top.*

*6-14. By the fifth crossing the pattern emerges, shown here on the underside of the seat.*

will be under 2 warp strands, over 3, under 3. Next, this same weaver is pulled over the right-hand rail to the underside of the chair. The weave now moves across the bottom. Turn the chair over and weave the splint back to the left-hand rail by weaving under 1 warp strand, over 3, under 3, and so on until you reach the left-hand side. If this same weaver is long enough it should continue around the rail to make a crossing on the topside of the chair seat (Figures 6-12 and 6-13). The third crossing is under 3 warp strands, over 3, under 3, and so forth. On the fourth crossing, go over only 1 warp strand, then under 3, over 3. The fifth crossing continues over 2 warp strands, under 3, over 3 (Figure 6-14). The sixth is over 3 warp strands, under 3, over 3. The seventh cross-

6-12.

6-13.

6-14.

*6-15. When half the weavers are completed, weave the fill-in warp strands. Note the loop at the back corner, where the splint is secured by tucking the end back into itself to the inside of the seat.*

ing is identical to the first, and the pattern repeats itself, starting at the left-hand rail: under 1 on the first crossing, under 2 on the second, under 3 on the third, over 1 on the fourth, over 2 on the fifth, and over 3 on the sixth crossing.

Weave the bottom in the same fashion as the top. You will alternate between the top and the bottom as the weaving moves toward the front of the chair.

To add a new weaver, instead of stapling a new length of splint as you did on the warp strands, simply weave a new strand by overlapping the old and new weavers 6 to 8 inches on the bottom of the seat. The tension of the weave will be sufficient to hold it in place.

When about one-half of the weavers are completed, start adding the fill-in warp pieces (Figure 6-15). These are woven parallel to the warp strands already in place.

Start at the right-hand rail and weave a 2½-foot length of splint parallel and adjacent to the existing warp, through the weavers and continuing the pattern already in progress. Secure this splint by tucking it around and under a weaver, under itself to the inside of the seat. This fill-in warp splint should be woven so that one edge is touching the existing warp and the other edge is touching the rail at the point of the tuck. It should not overlap either of these points but fit as neatly as possible, and go as far back into the gusset as it can be woven. (The gusset is the unfilled space at the corner of the chair.) Pull the other end over the front rail. Weave it through the weavers on the underside of the seat, continuing the pattern.

Add fill-in pieces in this fashion until the entire front rail is filled. Stagger each fill-in splint to continue the herringbone pattern.

With the fill-in splints in place, continue with the weavers until the entire seat is woven. Tightly weave the end of the last weaver against the front rail on the bottom of the seat with the aid of a flat-bladed knife (Figure 6-16).

FINISHING

When the seat is complete (Figure 6-17), clip or singe the little fiber hairs sticking up. Then mix 1 part boiled linseed oil with 2 parts paint thinner and brush the mixture onto the seat to protect the new splint (Figure 6-18). Flat reed gets brittle and should be oiled once a year to keep it limber. As the seat is used, however, it will sag some and reveal the unstained areas of the intersecting splints.

## Variations:
## Hickory, Oak, and Ash Splint

The chair shown in Figure 6-21 is woven with hickory bark in the Herringbone pattern just illustrated. The top and bottom of hickory are often confused: the lighter colored, rougher side is the correct (or "show") side and should face outward in the finished seat. This side was the closest to the outside of the tree. As the hickory splint dries, it will curl toward the darker, cambium layer. By facing this side toward the inside of the seat, you let the chair rails help counteract the splint's tendency to curl and therefore help keep the splint flat. The top, rougher side,

6-16.

**6-16.** *Guide the last weaver into place on the bottom of the seat with the aid of a flat kitchen knife.*
**6-17.** *The finished chair.*
**6-18.** *Oil the new splint with a mixture of 1 part boiled linseed oil and 2 parts paint thinner.*
**6-21.** *A seat woven with hickory splints.*

once sanded and oiled, shows the fine hickory grain to its best advantage.

Hickory, ash, and oak can be woven into any of the patterns detailed in this chapter. These woody splints do, however, require somewhat more care in the choosing of the materials and the weaving. Consult the materials chart at the beginning of the chapter for additional information.

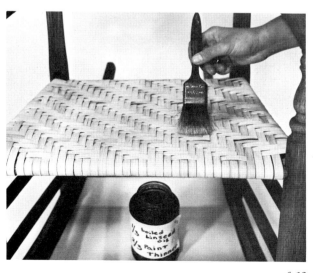

6-18.

6-21. 93

6-17.

6-22.

*6-22. Add a new hickory splint by interlocking the two ends with an arrow joint.*
*6-23. An arrow joint is used to join the old and the new ends of hickory or ash and other woody splints.*
*6-24. Continue warping with the new length. Always place the joint on the bottom of the seat with the arrow facing inside.*
*6-25. Half the weavers (in this case, hickory splints) are now finished. It is time to add the fill-in pieces.*

Splints of hickory, oak, and ash are traditionally joined with a special arrow joint. To make one, cut a small rectangle in one end of a splint and an arrow in the end of the new splint. Pass the tip of the arrow on the new splint through the rectangle, cut out of the end of the old splint. This will lock the 2 ends in place. Joined ends should always fall on the bottom of the seat, with the arrow facing toward the inside of the seat (Figures 6-22 through 6-25).

Figure 6-19 shows an alternative way to warp a chair, one that also makes the inserting of the weavers a little easier. But the pattern is not as strong as the herringbone because there are not as many warp strands connecting the front and back rails (Figures 6-19 and 6-20).

Another variation is the Diamond pattern, achieved by carefully graphing out the motion of each weaver (Figure 6-26). Counting each successive row of weavers takes considerable time but the resultant effect makes an interesting pattern (Figures 6-27 and 6-28).

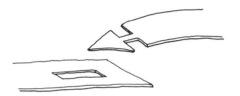

6-23.

6-24.

6-25.

6-19. Another pattern for setting up the warp strands. Pairs of warp strands are staggered on both top and bottom by wrapping the warp once around the rail between each pair.

6-20. A finished chair in which the weavers and the warp have been woven in pairs.

6-26. An example of the diamond pattern woven with ½-inch flat reed and colored with a dark stain.

6-27. Chair back with 4 diamonds in ash splint.

6-28. Another example of a diamond pattern, this one woven with 5mm binder cane and stained dark.

*6-19.*

*6-20.*

*6-26.*

*6-27.*

*6-28.*

**6-29.** *The finished Shaker rocker.*

## SHAKER TAPE WEAVING

Shaker tapes are heavy, woven-cotton webbing. The Shakers have used them on chairs of their own design since the 1830s. Shaker tapes are woven on small looms with dyed-cotton threads. They come in a variety of colors, are easy to work with, and, since they stretch only marginally unlike most woven fabrics, make a unique functional seat (Figure 6-29). The tapes can be used on the same pieces that take splint and rush.

### TOOLS AND MATERIALS NEEDED

*Needle*
*Thread*
*Scissors*
*Cotton tapes*
*Foam cushion*
*Carpet tacks, #3*
*Hammer*

Shaker tapes are available in widths of ⅝ inch and 1 inch. To determine the amount of material you need, consult the splint materials chart on page 88. Unlike splint, cotton tape is not available in a ½-inch width.

### WEAVING

Cotton tape is worked in much the same fashion as splint except that it is woven around a foam cushion and sewn together instead of stapled. Originally the Shakers used cotton batting, in contrast to the synthetic foam in common use now. The chair shown in Figure 6-29 is woven in a checkerboard pattern on the top and a herringbone pattern on the bottom. (The Checkerboard pattern is traditional for Shaker tapes; it can also be applied to splint, although it is not common.) The Herringbone pattern is used on the underside of the seat, simply because it is a faster pattern to weave than the checkerboard and the underside is rarely seen.

### Step One

First tack the end of the tape to the left-hand rail near the back corner. Wrap the tape around the front and back rails to form the warp. Insert the 1-inch thick foam cushion when the warp strands are approximately half done (Figure 6-30).

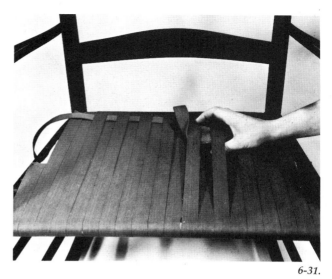

6-31.

6-30.

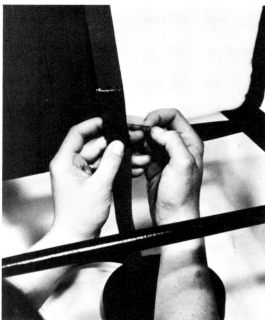

6-33.

6-32.

6-30. When the warp is one half finished insert the 1-inch foam cushion and continue warping.

6-31. To weave the checkerboard pattern, work the weavers over 1 warp, under 1, over another, and so forth. Coil the tapes for easy weaving.

6-32. Add a new length by sewing the ends of the 2 pieces together with a two inch overlap.

6-33. Add new weavers on the underside of the chair seat.

### Step Two

Begin the strand on the bottom by sewing it to one of the warp strands on the underside of the chair seat. Weave across the bottom, then bring it to the top of the seat. Work the weavers, first going over 1 warp, under 1, over 1, and so on (Figure 6-31). This tape continues around the rail to the underside, where it can be woven in either the same pattern or the herringbone (see pages 86 to 95).

The second crossing on the topside goes under 1 warp strand, over 1, under 1, and so on to the opposite rail. The third crossing repeats the pattern of the first.

Add additional tapes by sewing them together, with a 2-inch overlap (Figure 6-32). Hold the fill-in warp tapes to the side rails by tacks neatly hidden under the weavers.

97

Secure the final weaver by either tacking it to the inside of the front rail or sewing to one of the warp strands underneath the seat (Figure 6-33).

## RAWHIDE WEAVING

In some areas, rawhide was often used as a seat covering due to the lack of natural rush and trees for splints. Leather and raw-hide have such a multiplicity of uses that this adaptation to furniture was quite natural and was quickly accepted as a solution to the scarcity of wood and other indigenous fibers. Most of these rawhide seats were woven in an open weave on the same style of chair suitable for splint or rush. They were—and are—quite durable and comfortable as well as easy to weave.

### TOOLS AND MATERIALS NEEDED

*Hammer*
*Screwdriver*
*Mat knife*
*Carpet tacks, #4*
*Rawhide*

Precut rawhide is hard to come by. You can, however, cut your own. If you do, make sure it is a good, thick hide rather than a thin one that would be used for a drum skin. The kind of hide found on shoes is appropriate.

Rawhide comes in one natural color. It can be dyed, although it is not a common practice on this type of rawhide chair. When you find cut rawhide, there is some variation in the length and width. The width can be trimmed if there is too much variation between pieces. Trimming is done with a sharp mat knife after the leather has been marked lightly with a pencil.

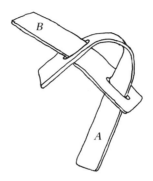

*6-34. A correct rawhide splice.*

For a mule-eared chair like the one shown, you will need 25 feet of thick, ⅜-inch-wide rawhide. Enough rawhide for one seat weighs approximately ½ pound. It is preferable to use one continuous length, but it is easy to splice another length as needed.

### PREPARATION

Soak the rawhide in hot (140 degrees F/60 degrees C) tap water for 4 to 5 hours. During this time it will stretch and become pliable, so much so that it should feel something like a long, slimy, limp noodle (Figure 6-34).

### WEAVING

The rawhide strand starts at the back right-hand corner and ends at the back left-hand corner. There are 7 loops on all the rails except the front, which has 6. The rawhide strand will always cross over itself after looping the rail (Figure 6-35).

**Step One**

Tack one end of the rawhide to the rear of the right-hand rail as you face the chair, so that the smooth side of the rawhide will face out and the pebbly, rougher side is against the rail (Figure 6-36). Wrap the rawhide once around the right rail to cover the tack, and then take it immediately to the adjacent back rail. Next, move the rawhide up through the space between itself and the back corner

**6-35.** *The rawhide starts at the back right-hand corner and ends at the back left-hand corner. There are 7 loops on all the rails except the front, which has 6 loops. The rawhide strand always crosses over itself after looping the rail.*

**6-36.** *Tack 1 end of the rawhide to the rear of the right-hand rail. The smooth side of the rawhide should be face out.*

**6-37.** *Bring the rawhide loosely to the front of the left side rail, around the rail, over itself, and directly to the adjacent front rail.*

**6-38.** *Use a mat knife to cut a slit where the new length of rawhide will be joined. Try to plan the splice where it will be least noticeable.*

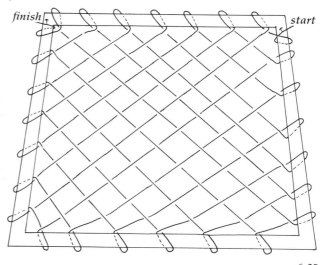

finish · start

*6-35.*

*6-36.*

*6-37.*

*6-38.*

post, then bring it over itself and in the direction of the opposite corner post.

Loosely weave the wet rawhide, then go back and pull it as taut as possible. It will stretch 10 to 25 percent when wet but will tighten as it dries, although not back to its original size. Weave quickly, as rawhide dries rapidly. Avoid twists, particularly on the rails.

**Step Two**

Bring the rawhide loosely to the front of the left rail, around the rail, over itself, and directly to the adjacent front rail (Figure 6-37). When new rawhide is needed, use a mat knife to cut a slit where the new length will be joined. The 2 ends are then spliced to-

99

6-39.

6-40.

6-41.

**6-39.** *Rawhide splice.*
**6-40.** *The rawhide splice pulled tight.*
**6-41.** *Slip the final tack under the last rawhide loop at the back left-hand corner.*
**6-42.** *The finished rawhide seat.*

6-42.

gether. Try to splice where it is least noticeable (Figures 6-38 through 6-40).

Continue weaving, forming the loops on the rails as you have done before. Follow the illustrations for the exact pattern. As you move to opposite rails, the rawhide strands will begin to cross over one another in the middle of the seat. You should cross each successive strand, first going over then under, over, under, and so on. When all the loops are completed, the end is tacked so that it is hidden under the last loop at the back left-hand corner (Figures 6-41 and 6-42).

Rawhide can be cleaned periodically with a damp cloth. A light coat of neat's-foot oil will refurbish cracked and dry rawhide. Be careful not to use too much, which will make the leather supple and therefore stretch your weaving.

# Danish Cord and Binder Cane

Danish cord is made in Denmark, and binder cane is the outer peel of the rattan palm. These products, although much different in appearance, have much in common. They have both traditionally been woven on the same Scandinavian style of chair, and are grouped together for that reason. The style of chair common to them is sometimes called Danish Modern, and has either a single or split rail, is made of a fairly high-quality wood, and has simple modern lines.

Danish cord is woven in a long length on L-shaped nails attached to the inside of the chair-seat frame. Binder cane comes in shorter lengths, usually of 10 feet or so, and is tacked to the chair frame. The actual weaving patterns used for both Danish cord and binder cane are quite similar, so skim this whole chapter before starting.

## DANISH CORD WEAVING

Danish cord is a heavy-duty, 3-ply twisted product. It has more body and is stiffer than fiber rush, but is not as suitable for rush weaving due to its tight twist. It cannot be worked in the same fashion as rush, which relies on the compacting of the individual strands for its strength. Fiber rush, by the same token, is not a suitable substitute for Danish cord.

Chairs with Danish-cord-woven seats are usually of 2 styles: those with a split or double side rail, and those with a single side

rail. Both are warped in the same fashion; it is the side to side weaving that is different.

While copies of Scandinavian chairs use tacks for changing the direction of the cord when weaving, the real Scandinavians utilize L-shaped nails to loop the cord around on the inside of the chair rail.

TOOLS AND MATERIALS NEEDED

*Hammer*
*Carpet tacks, #3*
*L-shaped nails*
*Clippers*
*Tack puller*
*Screwdriver*
*Needle-nose pliers*
*Danish cord*

Three-ply Danish cord, which is 4/32 inch in diameter, is available as either "laced" or "unlaced." Laced Danish cord has individual plies that are tightly twisted so that the cord resembles and has the texture of braided rope. Unlaced Danish cord has individual plies that are not so tightly twisted. The plies blend together more homogeneously when twisted and produce a smooth surface. Although Danish cord only comes in this one size, it is available in 2- or 10-pound coils. The average chair, like the one shown in Figure 7-1, requires 400 to 500 feet of Danish cord.

PREPARATION

Look over your chair carefully. Count the number of warp pairs (there should be an odd number) and the number of wraps between the warp pairs on the front and back rail. Mark on the chair where the warp pairs are. Record all this information for later use.

If the chair you are repairing has no seat left, try to visualize where the warp pairs were before the seat deteriorated. Their locations are sometimes noted by a faded finish etched with dust or grime. The L-shaped nails are also a reference to the warp pairs.

Loosen the L-shaped nails, but *do not remove them.* You may remove any tacks or wire nails that are anchoring the cord ends of the old seat. If your chair has no L-shaped nails, carefully study how the cord is applied.

Once your notes are made and you have traced the weaving pattern for all its quirks, remove the old seat and clean the chair. Any structural or cosmetic repairs to the seat

frame or the rest of the chair should be made now.

WEAVING

The following method of warping uses the cord directly off the spool. It is not necessary to cut off a smaller length or coil.

**Step One**

With this method, set up the warp strands then wrap separately the space between the pairs of the warp strands on the front and back rails. (Figure 7-1).

Study the illustrations carefully. Working from the spool, pull the end of the cord up under the chair and tack it to the inside of the front rail on the left side. The cord is hanging down now from the inside of the chair. Pull the cord up over the front rail to the back of the chair, and around the back rail, and then loop it around the first L-shaped nail on the left side of the back rail (Figures 7-2 and 7-3). Bring the cord back under and around the rail to the front rail. Take the cord over and around the front rail, loop it around the first L-shaped nail, and then pull it back under and around the front rail to the back. Loop it around the back rail and around the second L-shaped nail on the back rail and bring it to the front again (Figure 7-4). There are now 2 pairs of cord along the left side rail. Here the tricky part begins.

Bring the cord over the second L-shaped nail *and* and third L-shaped nail, so the cord is looped over both nails at once (Figure 7-5). Take the cord around the front rail to the back rail. Pull the cord around the back rail and around the L-shaped nail in a counterclockwise direction this time, coming back to the front rail *between* the double pair of cords and the single cord just strung to the back (Figure 7-6). Pull the cord over the front rail between these cords and then loop the cord over the third and fourth L-shaped nails (Figures 7-7 and 7-8).

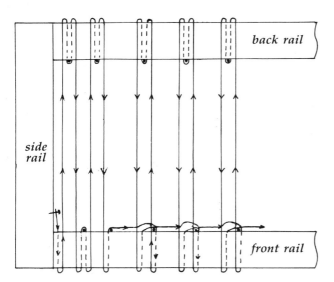

**7-1.** *The warping pattern for Danish cord.*

**7-2.** *Tack the cord to the inside of the front left corner and then pull it underneath and over the top of the front rail.*

**7-3.** *Loop the cord around the L-shaped nail on the back rail and then move back to the front rail.*

**7-4.** *At the front left corner, loop the cord around the first L-shaped nail and continue directly back to the back rail.*

**7-5.** *At the front left corner, loop the cord over the second and third L-shaped nails before moving to the back rail.*

**7-6.** *At the back rail, loop the cord around the L-shaped nail in a counterclockwise motion. Take the cord back to the front rail inside of the previous strand.*

**7-7.** *Take the cord back on the inside of the previous strand to complete the first spaced warp pair.*

**7-8.** *As before, loop the cord over two L-shaped nails and then go over the front rail to start another spaced warp pair.*

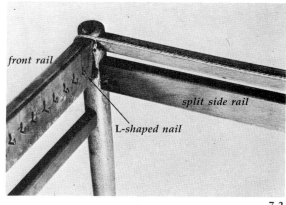

7-2.

7-3.

7-4.

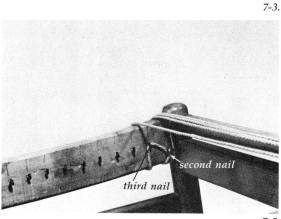

7-5.

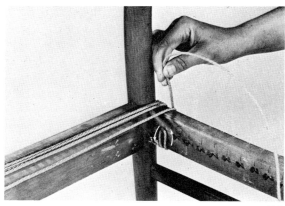

7-6.

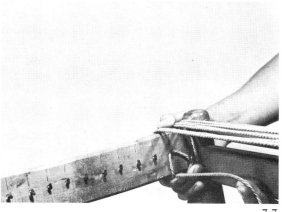

7-7.

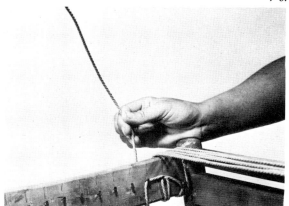

7-8

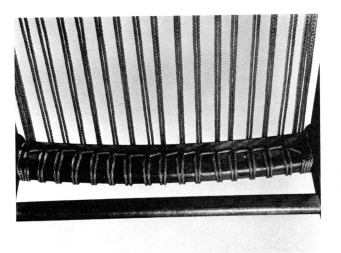

7-9.

7-10.

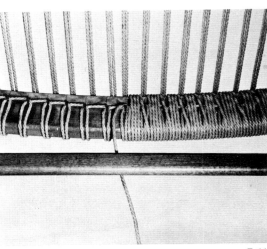

7-11.

7-12.

*7-9. The inside of the front rail at the completion of the warp strands.*
*7-10. To wrap the front rail, loop the middle of a 40-foot piece of cord over the center L-shaped nail on the front rail.*
*7-11. Working one end at a time in opposite directions, wrap the two ends around the front rail. There should be 3 to 5 wraps between each pair of warp strands.*
*7-12. The front rail is warped and wrapped.*

Continue this process to an odd number of warp strands (Figure 7-9). When the warping is completed, tack the end of the cord to the inside of the front rail on the right side.

**Step Two**

To wrap the front rail, pull and cut off 35 to 40 feet of cord. Loop the middle of the cord over the middle L-shaped nail on the inside of the front rail (Figure 7-10). Working with one end at a time, wrap the cord around the front rail in the spaces between the pairs of warp strands (Figure 7-11). Refer to your notes on the original seat to determine how many wraps occur in each space. There are normally 3 to 5 wraps per space on the front rail (Figure 7-12).

With another piece of cord 30 to 35 feet long, wrap the back rail. On the back rail there are usually only 2 to 4 wraps between pairs of warp strands.

104

7-14.

7-13.

*7-13. The front and back rails are wrapped, and all fifteen warp pairs and the 2 double warp pairs are in place.*

*7-14. Start the weft by making a double strand to form a pair of weavers. Bring the pair of weavers up and over the left side rail and weave across the seat, over, under, and over the warp.*

*7-15. Work the first pair of weavers over the double warp pair, and then in an under, over, under pattern.*

7-15.

Hammer in the L-shaped nails on the front and back rails to secure the cord loops (Figure 7-13).

### Step Three for Split-rail Chairs

The weavers, strands that run perpendicular to the warp, are woven from side to side in an alternating over, under, over, under pattern. When weaving the split rail chair, you must cut a length of cord; you cannot work directly from the spool.

Pull and cut off 50 feet of cord. Tack both ends on the inside of the left-hand rail, next to the back corner. Since this is a split-rail chair, you should tack them to the lower portion of the rail. Find the middle of the cord and weave with this double strand.

Pull this pair of weavers under the left-hand rails. Then go around both rails and over the top rail. Weave this pair over the double pair of warp strands that are adjacent to the left-hand rail and under the first single pair of warp strands (Figure 7-14). Then weave over the next warp pair, under the next pair, and so on to the right-hand rail (Figure 7-15). At the right-hand side, move the weavers over the double pair of warp strands. This is why it is important to have an odd number of warp strands: they allow the weavers to end the way they started.

Each time you reach the right-hand rail, bring the pair of weavers over the top of the rail and down the outside of both parts of the split rail. Then pass the weavers underneath the lower rail, and through the split in the rail over the top of the lower rail (Figure 7-16).

(Keep the cord tight when going around the side rail, but allow a little slack in the cord as it traverses the seat area. Allow only enough slack, however, to give contour to the seat.)

*105*

7-16.

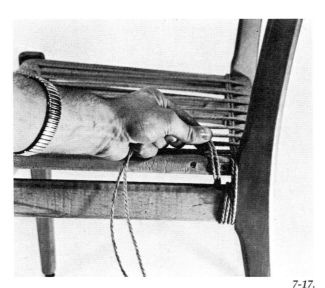

7-17.

7-18.

7-19.

**7-16.** *At the right-hand rail, take the weaver down the side and wrap it once around the bottom half of the split rail.*

**7-17.** *Bring the weavers up from the inside, through the slot in the split rail, and then up over the top to cross the seat again.*

**7-18.** *This is the left-hand rail. It looks like the right-hand rail but the procedure is different. On the left-hand rail, the pair of weavers go over the top, through the split, and once around the bottom half of the split rail.*

**7-19.** *After wrapping the bottom half of the split rail, bring the weavers up the side and over the top to start another crossing.*

Next, pass the weaver around the bottom half of the split rail, through the slot again and up, over the top of the right-hand rail, completing the wrapping on that side for that course (Figure 7-17).

To begin the second course, pass the weavers *under* the double pair of warp strands adjacent to the right-hand rail. Weave them in an over, under, over pattern. End by going under the double pair at the left-hand rail.

Each time you reach the left-hand rail, bring the weavers under the double pair of warp strands that are adjacent to the left-hand rail. Pass them over the top of the rail, halfway down, and *through* the slot to the inside. Pass the weavers around the bottom of the left-hand rail, up the outside, and back through the slot (Figure 7-18). This forms a wrap around the lower half of the split rail. Take the weavers around the bottom of the rail again, up the outside across both parts of the split rail, and over the top of both the rail and the double pair of warp strands (Figure 7-19). Weave across the seat as before.

The pattern for the right and left rails always remains the same as was woven on

**7-20.** *The completed chair.*
**7-21.** *A Scandinavian chair with a single side rail.*
**7-22.** *Bring the weaver across to the opposite side in the form of a loop.*

that rail previously. Tack the end of the cord to the inside of the rail when the weaving is finished or when you need to add another length of cord (Figure 7-20).

## Step Three for Single-rail Chairs

If your chair has a row of L-shaped nails on the side rails, you may weave directly off the spool without cutting a separate length.

The weavers on a single-rail chair with L-shaped nails (Figure 7-21) are quite easy to do. You may start at the front and weave toward the back, or start at the back and weave forward. In this example, the weaving is started at the front.

Tack an end of the Danish cord to the inside of the left-hand rail next to the front corner. Pull about 3 feet of cord under the left-hand rail. Take this length and form a loop. Essentially what you are doing is doubling it. This makes the weaving go twice as fast because instead of weaving just 1

7-20.

7-21.

7-22.

7-23.

*7-23. The double row of L-shaped nails is common to many single-rail Scandinavian chairs. The nails are staggered for close weaving, and some weavers double up on one nail.*
*7-24. Tack the trim strip perpendicular to the 2 fill-in pieces.*
*7-25. The completed chair.*

When the weaving is finished, tack the end of the weavers to the inside of the nearest rail and cut off the excess cord (Figure 7-24). Use every L-shaped nail on the side rails. Occasionally the loops will double up on an L-shaped nail. Use the hammer and screwdriver to compact the weavers on the side rail and keep them in line with the hooks being used (Figure 7-25).

## BINDER CANE WEAVING

Many Scandinavian chairs have seats woven of 5mm binder cane. They are often woven in the same patterns used for Danish cord, but their finished appearance is quite different. The chair shown here is a split-rail chair, and the pattern is essentially the same as the one shown earlier for cord seating.

7-25.

strand across the seat, you weave 2 strands, in the form of a loop, across.

Take the loop, or pair of strands, over the left-hand rail, then over the double pair of warp strands (Figure 7-22). Next take it under the first single pair of spaced warp strands, over the next pair, and so on, until you reach the right-hand rail. Then bring the loop over the double pair of strands adjacent to the right-hand rail, and over, around, and underneath the right-hand rail. Hook it on the L-shaped nail on the inside of that rail. After the loop is hooked, pull the cord taut from the other side of the chair. By weaving the loops across and hooking them on the opposite rails, you can work directly from the spool of cord without having to cut off specific lengths.

Continue the pattern at the left-hand rail. Bring the loose strand underneath the left-hand rail and loop it around the hook found there. Once it is hooked on the inside of the left-hand rail, pull it out to make another loop. Pull the new loop up over the top of the left-hand rail, *under* the double pair of warp strands, over the next single pair, and so on across the seat until the end, where it goes under the final double pair. Then bring the loop around the right-hand rail and hook it on the L-shaped nail (Figure 7-23).

Repeat the pattern again, first going over the double pair of warp strands, then under on the next course across.

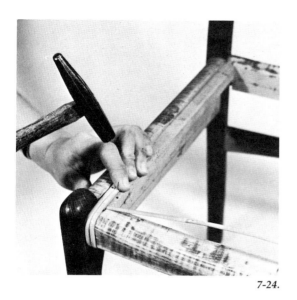

7-24.

Because of the nature of the material, however, there is a number of differences. The first is that binder cane is flat and has a glossy topside, whereas cord is round and has no one "correct" side. And unlike cord, which comes on a spool in almost any reasonable length, binder cane is made in lengths of 10 to 20 feet.

The second difference is that instead of L-shaped nails to hook the cord to, the cane is attached directly to the rail with wire nails. Finally, there are often several important trim strips that are inserted in the cane pattern along the front and back rails that are not present in the cord seat, as well as a decorative strip of either 5mm cane or small-diameter round reed that runs parallel to the bottom half of the split side rail.

## TOOLS AND MATERIALS NEEDED

*Tack hammer*
*Screwdriver*
*Clippers*
*Needle-nose pliers*
*Ruler*
*Pencil*
*Wire Nails, ½ inch × 20 gauge*
*Binder cane*
*Four lengths of split rattan, 5/16-inch diameter and 16 to 20 inches long (these lengths are often found on the chair)*

## PREPARATION

Weaving binder cane is done in fits and starts, as you are always tacking, pulling, weaving, adjusting, and so on.

Careful note should be made of the general flow of the existing weaving pattern. Inevitably, each chair will have a slight variation at one point or other, so while you are removing the old seat take note of how it was woven before. Any structural or cosmetic repairs to the chair frame should be made now, before the weaving starts.

## WEAVING

Soak the binder cane in hot tap water, (140 degrees F/60 degrees C) half an hour. This will make it pliable and easy to weave. Always weave with the glossy side of the cane facing out.

### Step One

On this chair, as is true of many Danish chairs several fill-in strips are needed to cover the rail near the front and back corners. Tack short strips of cane to the top of the side rail, wrap (Figure 7-24) around the front rail, and tack on the inside. When all the fill-in strips are in place, tuck 1 trim strip in place along the front rail and 1 strip along the back rail. The trim strip, which keeps the warp strands from shifting and rubbing on the rail edge, should be as long as the rail space it will cover. The seat will last longer with them than if no strips were used. How they work is a mystery. But they do!

With a pencil, mark the centers of both the front and back rails. Because the back rail is invariably shorter than the front, the space between the warp pairs will be smaller on the back rail. The front rail will, therefore, require more wraps between the warp pairs than the counterpart back-rail spaces.

Marking the center of both rails will help you maintain the symmetry of the spaced

109

7-26.

*7-26. Tack the first warp strand in place on the inside of the front rail.*

*7-27. Two warp strands have been brought across and tacked in place. Note that the trim strips go under the wrap and over the pair of warp strands, a pattern that they will continue throughout the weaving.*

warp pairs. Gauge the space and number of wraps between the warp pairs so that you reach the center of the front rail at the same time you reach the center of the back rail. The number of wraps on the front rail will vary from 2 to 3; the number of wraps on the back rail will vary from 1 to 2. There should always be at least one wrap between each warp pair.

### Step Two

Take a length of cane, glossy side up, and tack it to the inside front rail 3 inches from the left-hand front corner (Figure 7-26). (Don't place the tack directly at the end of the cane, or the cane will split.) Pull the cane around and over to the top of the front rail and *under* the decorative trim strip. Pull the cane across

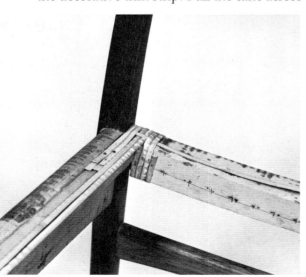

7-27.

to the back rail, under the trim strip, and around the back rail. Tack it to the inside of the rail.

Take another strip of cane and tack it to the inside of the front rail next to where the first one was tacked. Repeat the process: over the front rail, under the trim strip, to the back rail, and under the trim strip on the back rail. Instead of tacking it to the inside of the back rail, wrap it once or twice around the rail and the trim strip. Then tack it to the inside of the back rail (Figure 7-27). In the chair here, it is wrapped around the rail twice. The wraps go over the trim strip on the back rail holding it in place.

Take another piece of cane, glossy side up, and tack it to the inside of the front rail next to the 2 previous strands. Wrap it, 2 or 3 times depending on your spacing, around the front rail and the trim strip (Figure 7-28). The chair in the photographs is wrapped twice, each time going over the trim strip just as the wraps on the back rail did.

Now take the cane under the trim strip and pull it across to the back rail, where it goes under the trim strip on the back rail. Tack it to the inside of the rail. This is the first strand of the second warp pair. Bring another strand across as before, to form a pair. Wrap a strand on the back rail, then on the front rail, and continue the process until the warps and wraps are finished (Figure 7-29).

*Remember to space the pairs so that you can reach the center of the back rail at the same time you reach the center of the front rail.*

*7-28. Bring the first strand of a warp pair across the space, around the rail, and under the trim strip. Tack it to the inside of the rail adjacent to the previous strand.*

*7-29. The warping is two-thirds complete. The number of wraps on the back rail varies between 1 and 2 to allow for the shorter length of the back rail and to keep the pattern accurate.*

*7-30. As the cane comes out of the slot, twist it 180 degrees to keep the glossy side face out.*

*7-31. The trim strip can be tucked in under the first set of weavers.*

7-28.

7-29.

7-30.

### Step Three

The weavers are set up essentially like those in cord seating, detailed in Figures 3-14, 3-15, and 3-16. Carefully read Step Three under the heading Danish cord, and then keep the following differences in mind.

The first is that with Danish cord you work 2 strands at a time; with binder cane, you have only 1 strand at a time. Second, when the cane comes up through the slot or down into the slot of the split side rail, it must make a *twist* in order to keep the glossy side of the cane facing out (Figure 7-30). (Recall that cord is round and has no top or bottom.) Remember always to twist in the same direction on each weaver. Finally, with cane there is often a decorative strip (Figure 7-31), either of 5mm cane or a small-diameter

7-31.

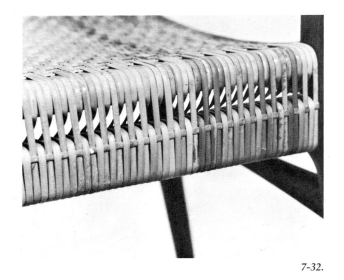

7-32.

*7-32. The finished side rail. The twists are all facing the same direction.*
*7-33. Add a new length of cane by tucking the new end under the wraps on the inside of the rail. (The old piece of cane can be seen running parallel to the inside of the rail.)*
*7-34. Cinch the old piece in place by passing the new piece through the slot and wrapping it once around the bottom half of the rail.*

round reed, running parallel to the bottom half of the split side rail.

To start, tack the cane to the inside of the side rail at the back corner. Follow Step Three under the heading Danish Cord. Essentially, the pattern is up the side rail and across the seat, weaving in an over, under, over pattern. Then it moves down the opposite rail, completely around the lower half, then around the lower half rail again and up through the slot to head back across the chair (Figure 7-32). *Don't forget that extra wrap around the bottom half of the side rail.*

To add another piece of cane, insert the new piece underneath the wraps on the inside of the side rail and cross the old strand over the new one (Figure 7-33 and 7-34). The new strand is held in place by the old wraps, and the old strand is held in place by the new wraps. This is an easier method than just tacking a new strand to the rail and is the common method of joining new strands of cane or reed when wrapping is involved. When the seat is finished, (Figure 7-35), tack the end of the last weaver to the inside of the side rail.

### Step Four

Nail a piece of half split rattan to the inside of the rails over the exposed nail heads (Figure 7-36). Besides hiding the nail heads, it also protects the ends of cane and sandwiches the split cane ends in place.

### A Variation for Single-rail Chairs

This example, a Scandinavian chair, has 4 single rails but with a thin slit running the

112

7-33.

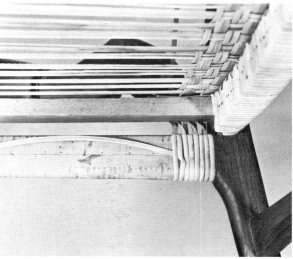

7-34.

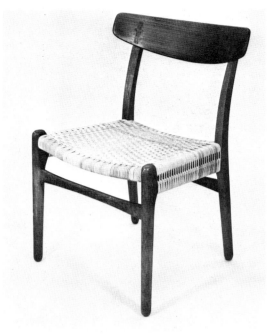

7-35.

7-35. *The completed chair.*
7-36. *Split a piece of rattan and tack it to the inside of all the rails to protect and cover the nail heads and to secure the wrapping.*
7-37. *For chairs with slits in their front and back rails like this Scandinavian chair, tack the warp on the top of the rail instead of on the inside, and pull the cane through the slit.*
7-38. *Wrap strand A around the rail and pull it through the slot. Tack strand B to the top of the rail and also pull it through the slot.*

length of the front and back rails (Figure 7-37). The cane seat must be woven through this slit and on the top half of the chair. Unlike the split-rail chair just detailed, the nails are on the top of the 4 rails, not on the inside of the rail. The nail head is then hidden by successive strands.

**Step One**

Examine Figures 7-38 through 7-41, and carefully read the captions. Use decorative trim strips and space the pairs of warp strands, but *work with 2 strands of cane at a time.* There

7-36.

7-37.

7-38.

7-39.

7-40.

*7-39. Strand A now covers the tacked end of strand B and has been pulled to the back rail. Strand B can be seen emerging from the slot.*

*7-40. Tack strand C to the top of the rail and pull it through the slot adjacent to strand B.*

*7-41. Strand B now covers the tacked end of strand C and is the second half of the warp pair. Strand C can be seen emerging from the slot. Wrap strand C around the rail several times to complete the cycle.*

should always be an odd number of warp pairs, as before.

Wrap strand A around the rail and then pull it through the slot. Tack strand B to the top of the rail and pull that also through the slot. Now pull strand A around to cover the tacked end of strand B. It then proceeds to the back rail. Tack strand C to the top of the rail and bring strand B around to cover it, just as strand A covered strand B before. Strand B is the second half of the warp pair, so bring it to the back rail. Strand C completes the cycle: use it to wrap the rail several times or as many times as called for in your pattern.

### Step Two

Because this is a single-rail chair, the weavers are set up differently than on a split-rail chair. They are also much easier to handle.

Tack a strand of cane to the top of the left-hand rail near the front corner. Pull the strand to the inside, around the rail, and over its tacked end; then cross it to the other side. Weave it through the warp pairs in an over, under, over pattern.

At the other side, pull the cane over and down the outside of the rail, underneath and up to the top again (Figure 7-42). Tack it adjacent to itself.

Follow the same pattern with the next strand (Figure 7-43). Starting at the left-hand rail, traverse the seat in the same over, under, over pattern you used with the previous weaver; go around the right-hand rail, cover the end of the first strand, and then tack it next to itself, Weave the next 2 weavers in the reverse order: under, over, under.

Continue adding weavers, alternating the pattern with every pair until you reach the back rail. When the seat is finished, tack the last weaver to the inside of the rail, as there will be no space left on the rail. Use the tack hammer and screwdriver to keep the strands adjusted and spaced evenly (Figure 7-44).

7-41.

7-42.

7-43.

7-42. *Tack the weavers to the top of the rail.*
7-43. *Each weaver hides the tacked end of the previous one.*
7-44. *The completed chair.*

7-44.

7-45.

7-45. *A classic chair, with 5mm binder cane.*

7-46. *To extend the woven seat over the chair rail, interweave the corners and attach the strands on top of the rail, underneath the weaving.*

7-47. *Weave strand B across the seat and around the side rail. Interweave it with the side warp strands around the side rail, where it becomes strand B as shown.*

7-46.

7-47.

**7-48.** *Nail strand B in place. Then cross strand A over the nail of strand B and interweave strand A around the side rail. Nail it adjacent to itself. Strand E will cover these 2 strands as you lay it in place.*
**7-49.** *The completed rattan chair.*

## Another Variation

On this chair as on the chair just described, each successive row of cane covers the preceding nail head. Examine the Figures 7-45 through 7-49.

To begin the warp, strands are anchored along the front rail only. The weavers (side-to-side strands), are woven through the warp strands along the front rail; in the example, they are woven in a diamond pattern. The warp strands are not anchored to the back rail until all the weavers are in place. The last half dozen weavers are woven at the same time to allow space for the anchoring nail on each warp strand. As shown, the warp strands are also nailed to the front of the legs so that they will cover the side rails. These nails will be covered by wrappings at the very end of the weaving process.

At the corners, the weaving strands are long enough to bend around and become the warp strands along the outside of the side rail. After the warp strands have been attached to the back rail, the sides are woven in one strand at a time, and nailed as shown in Figures 7-47 and 7-48.

# Wickerwork

The term wicker is used loosely to describe a number of kinds of woven furniture. Wicker commonly brings to mind the fancy Victorian rocker or settee in the sun room, but technically it includes not only rattan reeds but also willow, split reeds, and, since the 1920s, paper rush. Because wicker is a generic term covering many different styles and materials, there are too many repair techniques to cover in just one chapter. We have therefore chosen some of the more exemplary techniques and problems to detail. To cover as wide as possible an area so that both amateur and professional will benefit, both structural and cosmetic wicker repairs are shown.

Rattan furniture generally uses only rattan peel for all but the structural members, while wicker furniture uses full-round or split-round materials and incorporates fancy loops, curls, rolled arms, and twists.

Wickerwork employs basketry techniques that are enlarged and adapted to the structure of furniture. As in basketry, there are spokes—the vertical supports or warp—and weavers—the strands running perpendicular to the spokes. The weavers are worked in twists or just woven over and under the spokes. Spokes usually end in being woven into braids.

Repairing wicker furniture is a most rewarding craft because you can watch your fingers transform, strand for strand, a derelict bundle of twigs into an intricately woven human nest. Your hands recreate movements that hands long ago mastered. Your wicker piece was originally woven by hand, for no machine twisted those reeds into place. Repairing and replacing broken spokes, weavers, braids, and wrapping keeps the traditional craft of wicker work alive today.

TOOLS AND MATERIALS NEEDED

*Hammer*
*Mat knife*
*Sponge*
*Bucket*
*Neddle-nose pliers*
*Small saw*
*White glue*
*Pruning shears*
*Wire nails (various sizes)*
*Round reed (various sizes)*
*Binder cane or flat oval reed*

The tools needed for your repair will vary from piece to piece. We mention only some of the more common tools utilized in wicker repair.

Materials will also vary tremendously. You may need 2 or 3 different materials, not to mention sizes of those materials, for a single piece. Always save samples of the materials you remove from furniture so that you can measure their widths or diameters; you can also take them with you when you purchase supplies, and match new materials closely to the old.

Round reed, sold in 1-pound coils, is available in a great variety of sizes. The following chart lists them according to their numerical designation, diameter, and approximate footage per pound, together with sizes of flat reed, flat oval reed, and rush that are available.

ROUND REED

| Size | Diameter (in inches) | Diameter (in millimeters) | Footage per pound (approximate) |
|---|---|---|---|
| 0 | 3/64 | 1 1/4 | 2200 |
| 1 | 1/16 | 1 1/2 | 1600 |
| 2 | | 1 3/4 | 1100 |
| 2½ | 5/64 | 2 | 900 |
| 3 | 3/32 | 2 1/4 | 750 |
| 3½ | | 2 1/2 | 600 |
| 4 | 7/64 | 2 3/4 | 500 |
| 4½ | 1/8 | 3 | 400 |
| 5 | 9/64 | 3 1/4 | 350 |
| 5½ | 5/32 | 3 1/2 | 325 |
| 6 | 11/64 | 4 | 200 |
| 6½ | 3/16 | 4 1/2 | 160 |
| 7 | 13/64 | 5 | 150 |
| 7½ | 7/32 | 5 1/2 | 120 |
| 8 | | 5 3/4 | 110 |
| 8½ | 15/64 | 6 | 105 |
| 9 | 1/4 | 6 1/2 | 100 |
| 9½ | 9/32 | 7 | 90 |
| 10 | 19/64 | 7 1/2 | 80 |
| 11 | 11/32 | 8 1/2 | 40 |
| 12 | 3/8 | 9 1/2 | 35 |
| 13 | 13/32 | 10 | 25 |
| 14 | 7/16 | 11 | 20 |
| 15 | 1/2 | 12 1/2 | 15 |
| 16 | 9/16 | 14 | 14 |
| 17 | 5/8 | 15 3/4 | 12 |

FLAT REED

| Width (in inches) | Footage per pound (approximate) |
|---|---|
| 3/16 | 400 |
| 1/4 | 370 |
| 3/8 | 265 |
| 1/2 | 185 |
| 5/8 | 120 |

FLAT OVAL REED

| Width (in inches) | Footage per pound (approximate) |
|---|---|
| 3/16 | 300 |
| 1/4 | 275 |
| 3/8 | 175 |
| 1/2 | 90 |
| 5/8 | 60 |

RUSH

| Width (in inches) | Footage per pound (approximate) |
|---|---|
| 4/32 | 250 |
| 5/32 | 210 |
| 6/32 | 195 |

PREPARATION

Often, before any cosmetic or decorative repairs can be made on a broken piece, there is a considerable amount of structural repair needed. This includes removing broken pieces, repairing cracked posts, and strengthening joints. Figures 8-1 through 8-7 illustrate some the basic joint repairs and reed twists.

Joint repair usually requires binder cane, several screws, and glue. A small hand-held electric drill can be used to start the screw holes. Screws should be countersunk flush with the rattan or wooden post. Binder cane

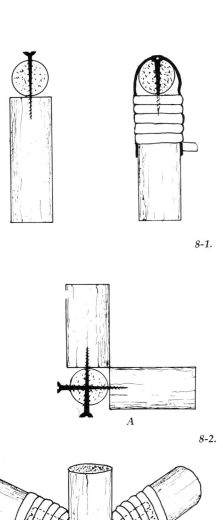

8-1.

8-2.

B

8-3.

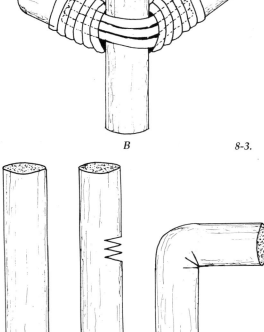

120     A          B          C          8-4.

8-1. *A single structural support, with screws and binder cane to hide the screw heads.*
8-2. *Structural corner support with screws.*
8-3. *Binder cane is wrapped around the joint to hide the screw heads.*
8-4. *A large piece of rattan can be bent more easily without heating if a saw-tooth cut is made at the point of the bend. Soak the rattan before bending it.*

is attached with Number 3 furniture tacks and glue. The binder both strengthens and visually enhances the joint (Figures 8-1 through 8-3).

Sometimes a large piece of rattan must be bent to be handled, as in Figure 8-4. There are several ways to do this. One is to soak it, make a saw-tooth cut in the rattan, and then bend it. Thick rattan should be soaked for at least 2 hours.

Larger rattan pieces can also be bent with applied heat; use a propane torch at the point you wish to bend it. (This method is also good for creating shallow curves.) If you use a propane torch, a standard or spreader nozzle is best, and the flame should move continuously over the surface of the rattan. The flame will be heating the inside of the curve, so wet the rattan to avoid burning its surface.

The 2 methods—cutting and heating—can be combined.

Wicker pieces often have decorative braids or twists around their edges, at the base of the apron or the inside of a rolled arm (Figure 8-6). These twists both make the piece visually interesting and serve to hold the spokes in place. A single arrow twist is often found strengthening the spokes on a chair back as in Figure 8-5a. A double arrow twist adds further solidity (Figure 8-5b).

## Interlocking Joint

A very common repair is the insertion of a single interlocking piece of reed between 2 broken ends (Figure 8-7). First, cut away wet broken reed ends to the point where they are sound. Then soak a new piece of similarly sized reed in warm water for an hour. Cut it to overlap about an inch on each side of the area to be filled. Then weave or splice the reed into place. The needle-nose pliers can be used to maneuver the reed.

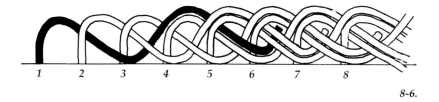

1 2 3 4 5 6 7 8

8-6.

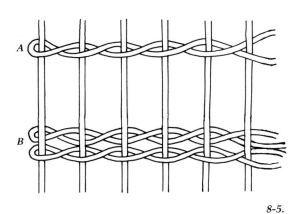

A

B

8-5.

## Double Reed Twist

Another repair technique often used is replacing a broken twist that ties spokes together. The chair illustrated in Figure 8-8 has vertical rattan posts and 4 double reed twists in an oak frame. The oak-and-reed combination is superb because the chair back is firm yet will "give." With normal use, the 2 middle reed twists broke at the right side near the post. And because of this, several of the vertical rattan posts popped out of the top frame member in the back (Figure 8-8).

To repair, first cut out the old reed twist. Put glue on the ends of the vertical reeds and re-insert them in their holes in the frame. Soak the reed in hot water until it is pliable. Then loop the middle of the new reed around the right-hand post. Weave the

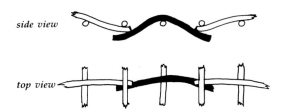

side view

top view

8-7.

8-5. (A) A single arrow twist. (B) A double arrow twist.
8-6. Double braid used to end spokes and often found on the inside of a rolled arm or in the base of an apron.
8-7. A short piece of reed locked into a hole caused by broken weavers.
8-8. An oak frame chair with a wicker back. The 2 middle twists have broken at the right side near the post, causing a number of vertical reeds to pop out of the top of the chair frame.

8-8.

8-9.

**8-9.** *Start the double twist by wrapping the middle of a single long piece of reed around the right post. Then weave the 2 resulting ends in and out of the vertical reeds, twisting the ends of the weavers each time they cross.*

**8-10.** *When you have reached the left-hand, side wrap the 2 ends around the post in opposite directions.*

**8-11.** *Wrap 1 end of the weaver around the left post twice. Altogether, there will be 3 wraps.*

2 ends of the reed in and out, almost like a snake crawls (Figure 8-9).

Twist the reed each time it crosses itself. At the left-hand side, pull the ends of the reed once around the post in opposite directions (Figure 8-10). Then circle the post again with the reed so that, altogether, there are 3 loops on the left-hand post (Figure 8-11). Return the 2 ends to the right-hand side in the same in-and-out pattern, twisting them each time they cross.

Wrap the ends around the right-hand post and insert them back into the double twist to lock them into place (Figure 8-12). Let the reed dry out, then clip off the excess (Figure 8-13). Leave enough so that when the chair back is stretched during use, the end won't pop out (Figure 8-14). About an inch of overlap is more than sufficient to secure the end of the reed.

8-10.

## Common Wicker Repairs

While the rocker in Figure 8-15 appears ready for the dump heap, it is really just in need of minor repairs, namely piecing the missing and broken pieces back into place. Patience is the key.

There are 3 major areas to be repaired: the back, the arms, and the apron. Following are good examples of wicker repairs typically required.

THE BACK

On this chair, the back has been severely pulled away from the top and side of the frame. To repair it, both new spokes (vertical reed) and new weavers (horizontal reed) are needed.

122

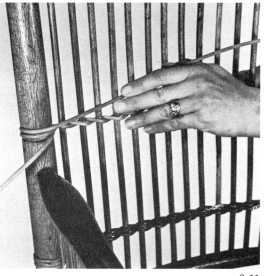

8-11.

**8-12.** At the right-hand side, wrap each end once around the post. Insert them back into the weave and pull tight.

**8-13.** Once the end is locked back into the weave, clip it off short—but not so short that it will pop out when the chair is stretched while in use.

**8-14.** The finished chair.

**8-15.** This damaged wicker rocker came into our shop with its back pulled away from the frame and the apron and arm rest in disrepair.

8-12.

8-13.

8-14.

8-15.

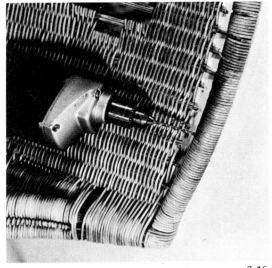

8-16.

8-17.

*8-16. With the rocker lying on its back, drill into the old holes in the frame to clear them and make room for new spokes.*
*8-17. With a mat knife, cut back the old spokes in the chair at staggered intervals.*
*8-18. Remove a damaged spoke with the aid of needle-nose pliers.*

Random cutting of spoke lengths increases the strength of the repair.

Remove the old spokes (Figure 8-18). Insert one end of a new spoke by manipulating it into the weavers (Figure 8-19). Cut off the other and insert it with some white glue into the chair frame (Figure 8-20). The frame is now ready to be wrapped with new reed.

Smear glue on the frame and wrap a new reed around it to cover the entire frame (Figure 8-21). Add the new reed in the same fashion as you would a new piece of binder-cane wrapping (Figures 8-44 and 8-55).

Tuck the new reed back under itself (Figure 8-22).

After the spokes are in place, the back has considerably more strength and the new weavers can be woven to finish the repair. Wherever the weavers are broken, cut them off and replace them. The pattern is generally over, under, over, with new-reed ends being locked into place under old reed ends. On this chair, the weavers start on the side, loop once around the post, and finish within the chair back. In this way both the side and

Soak the new reed for the spokes, the weavers, and the wrapping in hot water until it is pliable.

The broken spokes are repaired first. The ones in this chair are set in pairs, with one spoke inserted into a hole in the frame and the other lying alongside the first but not inserted into the frame. With a bit exactly the size of the new spoke, drill into the holes containing the old spokes (Figures 8-16). A tight fit is essential.

Next, saturate the part of the chair back needing repair with hot water so that no further damage will occur during repair.

Remove the old wrapping on the frame and cut the broken spokes at staggered points within the chair back (Figure 8-17).

8-18.

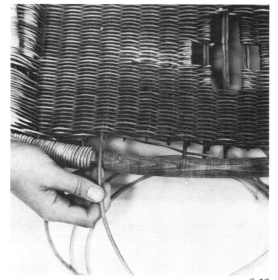

8-19.

**8-19.** *Insert a new spoke into the weave until it meets the point where the old spoke was cut.*

**8-20.** *After the new spokes have been inserted into the weave, pull the back up tight and glue the new spokes into their holes.*

**8-21.** *Smear the frame with glue. Soak reed in hot water and wrap it around to cover the frame.*

**8-22.** *When the wrapping reaches the point where the old reed begins, tuck the end of the new reed back under its last two wraps. Then pull it tight and clip it off short. When dry the joint will be secure and barely noticeable.*

**8-23.** *Secure the new weavers with a locking splice placed under a spoke in the side of the chair.*

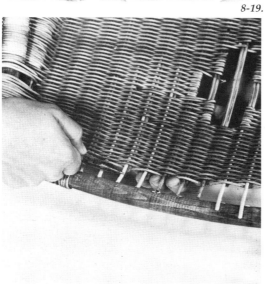

8-20.

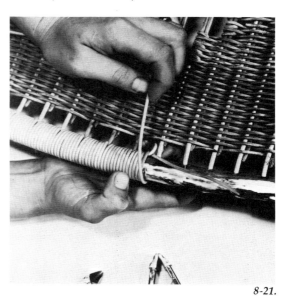

8-21.

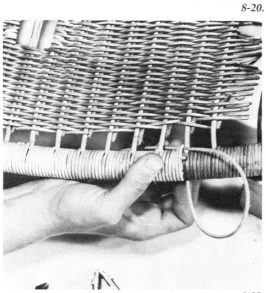

8-22.

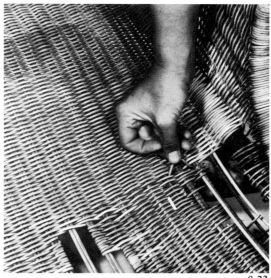

8-23.

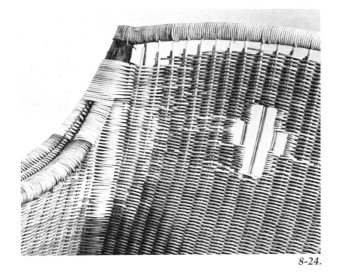

8-24.

**8-24.** *The weavers on the chair back are nearly complete. Only the space at the top of the chair remains to be filled.*
**8-25.** *The back of the rocker shows the newly spliced weavers. Note that the last bit of space at the top edge of the chair has been filled with a twist instead of the normal over, under pattern of the other weavers in the back of the chair. This same twist is echoed in the apron at the bottom of the chair.*
**8-26.** *To decorate the corner of the arm rest, place overlapping pieces of reed at right angles. Tuck them under existing old reed or tack them with wire nails.*
**8-27.** *Tie loose ends to the side of the arm rest. They will be covered by wrapping later.*

the back of the chair are repaired at the same time (Figures 8-23 through 8-25).

### THE ARMS

Work needed on the arms and arm rests is generally cosmetic. However, before starting, check all the joints for strength.

To begin the repair, cut back the old reed from the damaged area and clean it away. Next, place the new pieces of reed at right angles, either tacking them down or tucking them under the remaining old reed (Figure 8-26). Stack the round reed at right angles so that when it is bent down to cover the post of the arm rest it forms a plaited corner. Then tack down the plaited ends and cover them with a wrapping of another piece of round reed, which should move in a circle around the post (Figure 8-27).

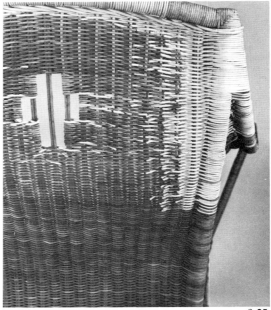

8-25.

8-26.

8-27.

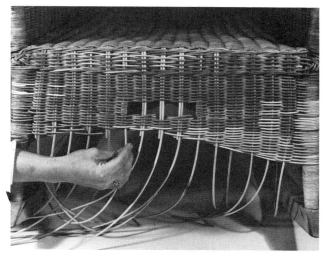

*8-28. When replacing the spokes in pairs leave 1 spoke long (with a tail of several feet), and cut off the other to match the general curve of the apron.*

*8-29. The braid at the bottom of the apron. The spokes cross in front of the 2 adjacent spokes and are then locked in place behind the third spoke.*

*8-30. To begin the triple twist, splice 3 pieces of Number 6 reed into the chair. Bring 2 pieces around the front of the leg and the third from behind.*

## THE APRON

On most chairs, if the apron is in need of repair it is at the point where it joins the chair seat at a right angle. If such is the case, new spokes are required; these will often continue around the edge into the seat itself. On the chair illustrated, most of the spokes needed to be replaced.

To replace spokes, first wet with hot water the entire area to be repaired. Cut off the broken spokes at staggered points within the seat, and replace them with new ones as you would with a chair back. Of each pair, leave 1 new spoke with a long tail and clip off the other at the bottom of the apron (Figure 8-28). Once the spokes are in place, tighten or replace the weavers as necessary.

To hold the weavers in place and create a finished border, weave in a 3-reed twist at the bottom of the apron. On this chair, the reed used for the twist is a size larger than that used for the weavers.

8-28.

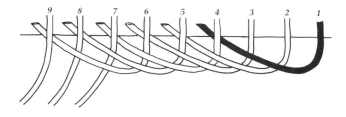

8-29.

### *Three-reed Twist*

**Step One**

Three pieces of, in this case, Number 6 reed are spliced into the apron on the right side of the chair. Bring 2 strands around the front of the chair leg and the third strand from behind (Figure 8-29). *Because* this is a restoration, the reed can be spliced into the twist already on the side of the chair.

For a completely new twist, tack the 3 reed pieces to the inside of the back right-hand corner post. Then bring 2 pieces around the outside of the leg, and 1 straight to the right side (Figure 8-30).

**Step Two**

Pull each strand of the Number 6 reed (now called weavers) in front of 2 spokes and behind 1 spoke, at the same time twisting it around the other 2 reeds each time they cross (Figure 8-31). Continue this pattern to the

8-30.

8-31.

**8-31.** *Twist each of the weavers over 2 spokes and behind 1 spoke, at the same time twisting it around the other 2 accompanying reeds each time they cross.*

**8-32.** *Splice the ends of the 3 reeds into the opposite side, with 2 reeds going around the front of the chair leg and one coming from behind.*

**8-33.** *To complete the final braid, start with the spoke farthest to the right. Weave it over the first 2 spokes to the left. Weave each successive spoke over 2 and under 1 until all the spokes are locked into place.*

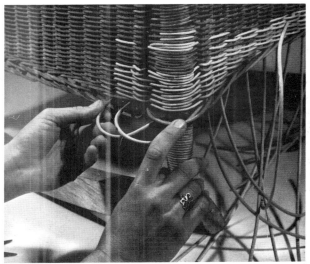

8-32.

opposite side, where you splice the reed ends into the apron on the left side. At the left leg, bring 2 reeds around the front of the post and 1 behind, as before (Figure 8-32).

Next weave the spokes into the bottom of the apron to finish the chair. Start the pattern at the spoke tail farthest to the right. Bring the tail over the next 2 spokes to the left, then lock it under the third (Figure 8-33). Clip off the excess reed. The next spoke is then picked up and follows the same motion, over two, under the third. The weaving continues until all the spokes are in place (Figure 8-34). The new, lighter-colored reed will soon age and match the color of the older reed.

## ROLLED ARMS

Repairing a rolled arm can very quickly give you the satisfaction of being an accomplished wickerworker! While it looks like you'll never get the curve right again, step-by-step replacement of the spokes and weavers will accomplish the task. The key is to replace a strand at a time. Don't start from scratch; let the existing curve define the curve that you will recreate.

First saturate with hot water the entire part of the arm that needs repair. This will make the reed pliable and easier to work.

Cut off the remains of the old spokes at the frame and remove them with needle-nose pliers (Figure 8-35). Then, using a drill bit exactly the same diameter as the new reed, drill holes where the old spokes were (Figure 8-36). The new reed spokes should

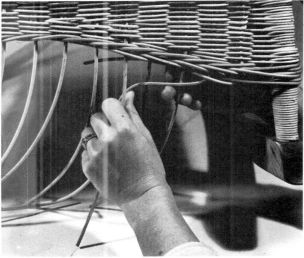

8-33.

**8-34.** *The finished chair.*
**8-35.** *Cut off the old broken spoke at the frame with a mat knife, and pull it out with needle-nose pliers.*
**8-36.** *Drill into the old holes to make room for the new spokes.*

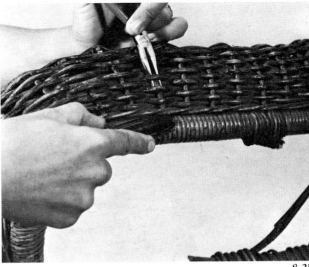

8-35.

8-34.

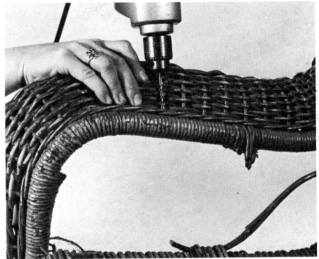

8-36.

fit snugly into the clean hole. Now insert the new spokes into the arm (Figure 8-37): hold the tip of the reed with a pair of needle-nose pliers and gently tap the pliers with a hammer to guide them into the weave. In this fashion, the reed end is easily maneuvered through the weavers (Figures 8-38 and 8-39).

Next put a moderate amount of glue into the holes of the frame and insert the reed ends. In this chair, the other ends of the reed spokes are left long and are later woven into the braid on the edge of the rolled arm (Figures 8-40 through 8-42). Your chair may be somewhat different. Examine it carefully and then follow the original pattern.

The arm should be kept thoroughly wet

and pliable throughout the repair process. Examine the old reed for broken or missing pieces. Remove any that is broken by clipping the reed weavers at the nearest place to the break where the reed goes under a spoke. If there are a number of broken reeds in one area, try to stagger the points at which they are cut.

Now weave the new weaver into place. First, lock it under the spoke where the broken reed ends. Then work it in an over, under, over pattern until it fills the empty space (Figures 8-43 and 8-44). It will end as it starts, by locking under the nearest spoke. After the reed is dry, it will be quite secure.

A decorative loop is placed (or replaced)     129

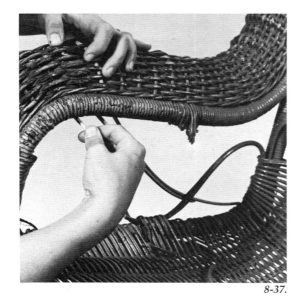

8-37.

**8-37.** *Now work new reed into the rolled area from the outside, going over the top and into the new hole.*

**8-38.** *Holding the reed end, gently tap the pliers with a hammer (but not hard enough to do damage) to pull the new reed across the top and into the hole.*

**8-39.** *Looking from the outside of the arm, 4 new spokes are in place.*

**8-40.** *To lock the tail ends of the spokes into the inside of the roll, bring the spoke on the right over the next 2 and under the third.*

**8-41.** *With the next spoke the pattern continues, going over two and under the third.*

8-38.

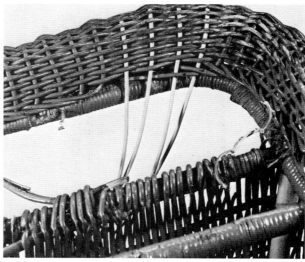

8-39.

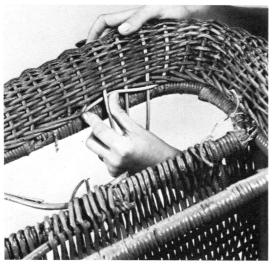

130

8-40.

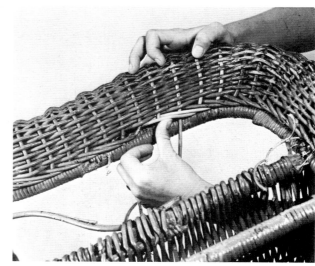

8-41.

*8-42.* Lock the last of the new spokes into place, completing the repair.

*8-43.* Add a new weaver by working through the new spokes in an over, under, over pattern.

*8-44.* The repaired arm. Several new weavers were enough to fill the space left by the broken ones.

*8-45.* A new decorative loop is placed in the space between the seat and the rolled arm. The loop will be held in place by both the old reed and some new wrapping still to come.

8-42.

in the space between the arm rest and the chair-seat frame (Figure 8-45). Do this by soaking the correct-size reed for 2 or 3 hours, then using a simple nail jig to hold the loop in its place until it is dry. (A nail jig can be set up on any scrap of wood or on a work-bench that you can nail into. Hammer nails into position so that they hold the reed in the shape you want. An example of a more complex jig is found under the heading Reed Chain Stitch, which follows.)

When the decorative loop is dry, remove it from its nail jig and install it.

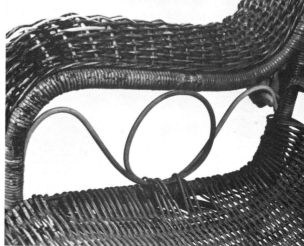

8-43.

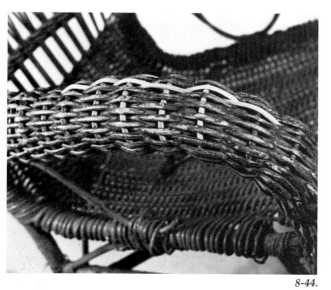

8-44.

8-45.

8-46.

## Reed Chain Stitch

And now for a little fun. Should you remove all the original chain stitch from the back of a piece such as the child's rocker illustrated in Figure 8-46, you could repair it with, for example, a simple twist or splint weave. But a fancy chain stitch is the experienced caner's answer! Notice that the wrapping on the chair just hides the reed ends and nails. The mistake one might make here is to wrap too soon, before all the chain rows are secured.

The rocker has an interlocking-chain-stitch back made from round reed. Through use and age, some of the reed has been broken and is in need of repair. The repair is done in 2 stages. First the chain stitch is replaced. Then the frame, which borders the chain stitch, is wrapped with new binder cane.

### Step One

Remove all of the old cane and reed from the back of the chair. Save a section of the old chain stitch to use as a pattern for the replacement chain. Make a mental or written note of the number of reed chains that are removed.

Set up a jig to form the reed stitch (Figure 8-47). (Keep an old piece of chain nearby to use as a pattern.) After soaking the new reed in hot water, arrange it on the jig and allow it to dry. It usually takes overnight for the reed to dry enough to hold its new shape.

*8-46. A child's rocker as it came into our shop, with several links completely missing and others broken enough to need replacing.*
*8-47. Use an old piece of chain stitch as a pattern for the new one. To make the chain stitch, fashion a jig from a board and short dowels.*
*8-48. Tack each loop of the first chain to the chair frame with wire nails.*

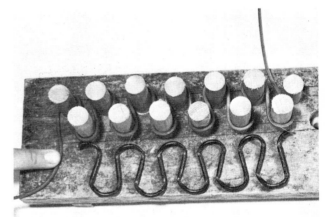

8-47.

8-48.

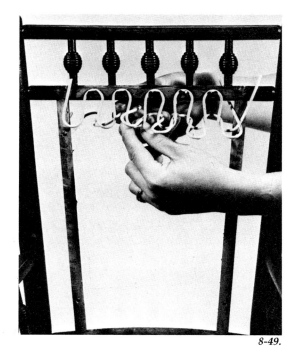

8-49.

**8-49.** *Slip the next chain stitch into place.*
**8-50.** *Once all the chains are in position, tack down the ends with the aid of pliers and a hammer.*
**8-51.** *Tack binder cane horizontally across the top and bottom of the chair frame. These strips cover the loops and keep the nails from slipping out through the wrapping.*

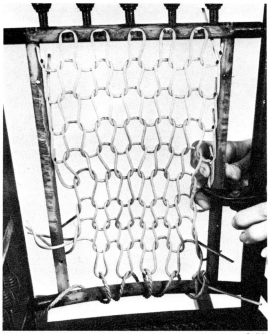

8-50.

The new reed chains will open slightly and have some spring.

Now you can attach the reed chain to the frame (Figure 8-48). Place the chain horizontally across the top of the frame and tack each loop to the frame with a ½-inch, 20-gauge wire nail. Insert the second row through the loops of the first row from behind the first row, being careful to align the loops through the proper links (Figure 8-49). Tack the ends of each chain to the sides after you loop the next chain into place. In Figure 8-50, pliers are used to squeeze the wire nail into place.

After 3 rows of chains are nailed into place, interlock the rest of the rows. Tie them temporarily to the sides so that the necessary pulling and stretching can be done to align the chains with the frame. Then using the pliers and wire nails, anchor the chains to the side rails and the bottom rail.

**Step Two**

When all the reed chains are in place, start the binder cane. First wet a piece of binder cane and tack it parallel to the top and bottom of the frame, on top of the nail heads (Figure 8-51). This cane strip keeps the loops and nails from popping out.

Next wrap the corners with binder cane

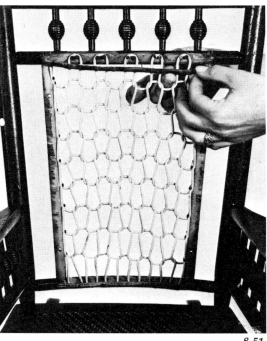

8-51.

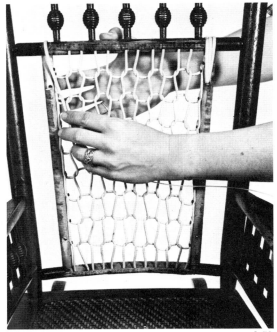

8-52.

8-52. Wrap the corners first, using the hole drilled in the frame.
8-53. Wrap the frame with binder cane.
8-54. Adding a new length of wrapping cane.

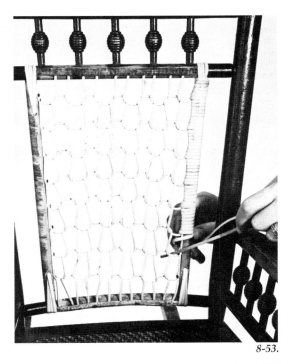

8-53.

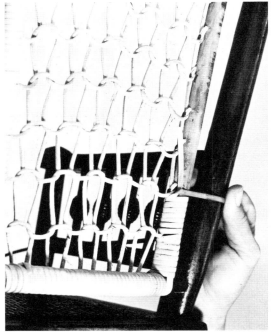

8-54.

(Figure 8-52), which will fill a space that would otherwise be left bare. The corners on the chair illustrated have a hole conveniently drilled for this special wrap. If your chair does not, nail the cane down.

Finally, wrap the rails (Figures 8-53 through 8-55). This both covers the rails with a fine border and doubly secures the reed chains that form the back of the chair.

To add another piece of binder cane when wrapping, insert the new piece underneath the wrap, on the inside of the rail. Cross the new strand over the old one. The new strand is held in place by the old wraps, and the old strand is held in place by the new wraps (Figure 8-55).

### Finishing

The chain stitch can be treated with varnish stain to match the rest of the chair and then sealed with a clear coat of lacquer, shellac, or varnish. The reed should be oiled after several years to keep it supple and pliable.

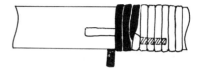

*8-55.*

*8-55. The wraps of the old binder secure the end of the new length of binder, while the new wraps secure the end of the old binder.*
*8-56. The finished chair back.*

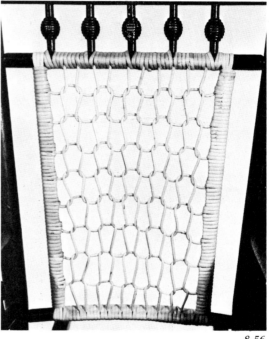

*8-56.*

# INDEX